LANCASTER AT WAR

LANCASTER AT WAR

Life in the city in World War Two

JOHN FIDLER

First published in 2018
by Palatine Books,
Carnegie House,
Chatsworth Road
Lancaster LA1 4SL
www.palatinebooks.com

The right of John Fidler to be identified as the author of this work has been
asserted in accordance with the Copyright, Designs and Patents act 1988

British Library Cataloguing-in-Publication data
A catalogue record for this book is available from the British Library

Paperback ISBN 13: 978-1-910837-16-0

Designed and typeset by Carnegie Book Production
www.carnegiebookproduction.com

Printed and bound by Jellyfish Solutions

CONTENTS

Note: fifteen photographs (identified as (LG/LCM) were published in the *Lancaster Guardian*, and are in the collection of the City Museum. They are published here by permission.

CHAPTER 1

LANCASTER IN 1937

To mark his coronation, King George VI (the Duke of Lancaster) conferred on Lancaster by Royal Charter on 14 May 1937 the status of a city. This, whilst an honour, made little real difference – Lancaster was the ancient County Town of what is properly called the County Palatine of Lancaster, and was the most important Assize town in the North West. Since the first Charter, conferred by John, Count of Mortain (soon to become King John) in 1193, she had been the market town for north Lancashire. Villagers in the Lune valley, in nearby Poulton-le-Sands, Bare (there was no Morecambe until 1850) and Heysham brought their produce in to the markets held each Wednesday and Saturday, and used the facilities offered by solicitors, tailors, booksellers and cinemas. Later charters conferred the right to send two members to Parliament, reduced to one by the Reform Act of 1867. The right to hold a horse fair twice a year had been a valuable asset when the horse was the sole means of transport. (The horseshoe at Horseshoe Corner, despite other, more romantic explanations, almost certainly records this important privilege.)

The first real industry in Lancaster was shipbuilding. In the seventeenth and eighteenth centuries, two shipyards on the Lune built vessels of up to 300 tons burthen, and the port traded with the West Indies, the Baltic and America as well as involvement in the coastal trade. From the Baltic came the naval stores of timber, turpentine, tar and resin, with flax for sailcloth and hemp for cordage.

With ships growing larger, and the Lune beginning to silt up, this enterprise lapsed after 1800, though Lancaster remained the port of registration for vessels whose centre was now Heysham.

The woodworking firm of Gillows had been making fine furniture (using the mahogany brought in from the new world) since 1728, and in the late nineteenth century had diversified into making panelling for town halls and ocean liners. (During the First World War there had been further diversification into making ammunition boxes, aircraft parts and even shell cases.) In 1937, however, the largest employers were Storeys and Williamsons, both established in the nineteenth century. Both families had contributed to the amenities of the city: the Storey Institute had been established in 1887 to provide a library, reading room and art gallery. James Williamson in 1880 paid for the landscaping of the old quarry to make a public park, and his son (ennobled as Lord Ashton) added to it the remarkable baroque creation, known locally as 't'structure', but more properly called the Ashton Memorial. A more practical purpose was served by the building of a new Town Hall in 1909, which provided not only a council chamber, but the fire station, police station, the police court (as the Magistrates' Court was then known) and a concert hall. Its eighteenth-century predecessor became the City Museum. Newer enterprises included Standfast, set up by Morton Sundour of Carlisle in the old Wagon Works on Caton Road, manufacturing dyestuffs, and the artificial silk firm of Lansil. As a result, the city's unemployment figures, even in the slump years of the 1930s, were well below the national average.

The Roman Catholic church of St Peter, built to the design of local architect E. G. Paley, became a cathedral in 1924 with the creation of a Roman Catholic diocese based in Lancaster. The Anglican Vicar of Lancaster, the Revd Benjamin Pollard, had in 1937 become Suffragan Bishop of Lancaster, assistant to the Bishop of Blackburn. To the medieval Priory Church of St Mary had been added in 1927 a memorial chapel for the King's Own Royal Lancaster Regiment, whose depot was at Bowerham Barracks (later St Martin's College, and now the Lancaster Campus of the University of Cumbria). Lancaster's schools will be dealt with in Chapter 10.

Since the end of the First World War there had been considerable developments in housing, with estates of council houses at Bowerham, Ryelands, Greaves, Skerton, Newton and Marsh (a total of almost 17,500), with consequent demolition of city centre slums. Private housing (much of it in the 'semis' typical of the 1930s) had also been built on the outskirts of the existing town. The Westfield Memorial Village had also been created for ex-servicemen – a bold vision of housing on land donated by Mr Herbert Storey. It was intended to have workshops and social facilities including a club and a bowling green, but trade union opposition prevented the building of the workshops. It had been opened in 1924 by Field Marshal the 1st Earl Haig.

The local shops such as the grocer T. D. Smith, Atkinson's Tea and Coffee Warehouse, and the jeweller Henry Little were in 1933 joined by Marks and Spencer and Woolworth. A new cinema, the Odeon, joined the older establishments, and the one theatre was the eighteenth-century Grand Theatre in St Leonardgate. The Royal Lancaster Infirmary, still a private charity (pending the creation of a National Health Service), was extended in 1924 and 1934.

CHAPTER 2

THE COMING OF WAR

THE year 1939 opened quietly enough. The principal events recorded in the two local papers, the *Lancaster Observer* (every Friday, 2*d.*) and the *Lancaster Guardian* (also every Friday, 2*d.* – 'read in four out of every five homes in Lancaster'), were the January sales. The local outfitters, Studholmes, Gorrills, Mansergh, Nuttall & Sinclair, Alfred Hinde and Sam Cooke, the schools outfitters Scott-Richmond, Reddrops, the furniture shop Waring and Gillow, and the jeweller and optician Leightons were all vying for business. The front pages of both newspapers were dedicated to advertisements and public notices, and for the rest offered only local

Guardian Nig-Nog Club

Nignog Birthdays

Birthday greetings to these Nignogs:—

July 6th: Jean Baines, Joan Holden, Hilary Clarke, Stanley Mason, John Brayshaw, Mary Norris.

July 7th: W. L. Greatorex, Veronica Waites, Alan Lambert, David Burrell, Brenda White Jean Hough

July 8th: Francis Tower, Maurice Townley, John Brown, Ernest Robinson, O. Lowther.

July 9th: Bernard Shenton, [illegible]

July 10th: Allen Wilkinson, F. Stokes,

July 11th: Veronica Smith

"Guardian" Nignog Club

Please Enter Me as a Nignog in the Children's Ring.

Name ....

Address ....

....

School ....

Age ....

Date of birth ....

Boy or Girl ....

Newsagent ....

.... 6/7/45

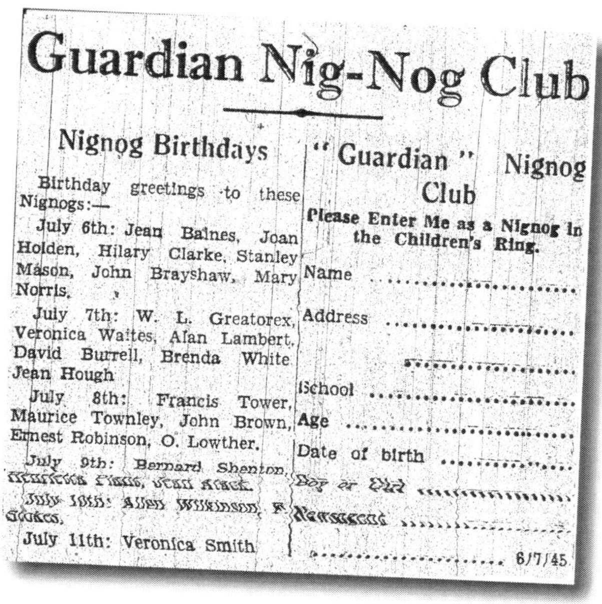

Extract from the *Guardian*

Madame Doreen Offers The LATEST NECK-LINE

FASHIONS change in neck-lines. Or do they really, when you come to think about it seriously?

Perhaps it is not only a question of fashion. There are practical considerations, that of comfort being by no means insignificant. Then, of course, the desire for change has more than a little influence, and sometimes we find that we wish to go back and revive a style about which we had almost forgotten.

Only the other day, for example, I observed that the tie-necked blouse has returned to favour. This is both comfortable and attractive. It is an easy style to make-up. So I have had one drawn for you, and here is the result.

The blouse has long sleeves, but if you prefer them short, cut the pattern just above the elbow, and, incidentally, you will save yourself just over a quarter of a yard of material.

You will find that this type of neck-line looks extremely smart between the revers of your suit. It is suitable for all times and all types of women. Most blouse fabrics are suitable, but my own preference is for a plain or very tiny spot patterning.

The pattern is available to you in a 34in., 36in., 38in., 40in., of a 44in. bust size, taking two yards of 36in. to 38in. wide material and half-a-dozen buttons.

To obtain the pattern, No. 31, and illustrated instructions for making, send P.O. value 1s. 3d. (which includes Purchase Tax) made payable to MADAME DOREEN. Address your application c/o the Magazine Editor, and state bust size required.

From the *Guardian*

news. Council meetings, the hearing of petty crimes in the police courts, accidents, weddings (with photographs), deaths and funerals, public appointments, sports results and news from the surrounding villages was their stock-in-trade. Agricultural news, gardening tips ('the uses of soot') and dressmaking hints, news of Scout and Guide activities abounded. The *Lancaster Guardian* had a Nig Nogs page for the children who had joined its Nig Nog Club (just children – no racial connotations then). Each was given a badge, their birthdays were recorded in the paper, and their letters published. It also featured a fashion column, in which 'Madame Doreen' depicted women's wear ('A dainty summer nightie', 'Your new spring

'ndie Patterns are Popular says Madame Doreen

There is no doubt about it. Whenever I offer an undie-pattern in this column whether it is for the school-girl, the young woman, or the matron there is an overwhelming response from readers. More and more women are obviously making their own lingerie.

This is not really surprising, because such dainty garments are well worth the time spent on them.

Another point, too, is that they are easily made by hand by those of you who are unfortunate enough not to possess a sewing machine. In response to a request from a reader, I am this week offering an undie-set with a difference. The opera top slip is cut on the bias and to complete the set there is a pair of directoire knickers.

French knickers are usually offered with this type of slip, so I hope you will approve the change. I feel sure you will, as except for the very young woman, directoire knickers seem to be popular.

The pretty floral lingerie fabric, as chosen by my artist to illustrate the sketch, makes a dainty set, but any of the plain pastel shades will make up equally well. Shoulder straps are suggested as being narrow, double bands of self, but you could use ribbon if preferred.

From the *Guardian*

suit', 'Dainty cami-knickers', 'fit for a princess' (a dress for a girl, in three sizes up to age six) or 'a blouse-dress, just right for remnants') with patterns available at 1s. Only rarely was there any mention of national, still less international items. The editor of the *Lancaster Observer* did print his 'Observations', and in the first issue of January offered a survey of the previous year. In January 1937 he had cited not only the celebrated case of Doctor Buck Ruxton, tried for the murder of his wife, but also recorded his disquiet at the Italian invasion of Abyssinia and the civil war in Spain. Early in the year there were collections in cinemas and the theatre for Lord Baldwin's Fund for Refugees. These were mostly those fleeing from Nazi Germany, from

Austria after Hitler's annexation of his native country, and from the horrors of the Spanish civil war.

Political meetings did raise other matters. Lieutenant Colonel W. C. Ross, the prospective Liberal candidate referred more than once to 'Britain's peril', though he was more concerned with Mussolini than Hitler. In January he asserted that 'Fascism knows no peace', with the disconcerting verdict that 'war is on the way', but then in May asserting that 'Hitler has overplayed his hand'. The prospective Labour candidate, at a party meeting in April, attacked the government, 'run by a frightened prime minister, whose supporters are now beginning to realise that Hitler was a blackguard'. At that time too there was concern in readers' letters about the introduction of conscription, which the prospective Labour candidate denounced as 'a first step towards Fascism'. An editorial note in May referred to the position in Palestine, and another in June quoted the Russian foreign minister Molotov's designs on the Baltic states. Again it was in readers' letters that a danger of war was raised. Elsewhere, large black headlines declared that 'AN EMERGENCY MAY COME ANY DAY' – however this was only an advertisement for the wireless relay system Rediffusion.

On 1 April, the city's new 'bus station on Damside', and 'bus depot at Kingsway' were opened. 'Contrary to expectations,' wrote the editor of the Observer in his 'Observations', 'the inauguration of the omnibus station, and the reorganisation of the traffic routes through the city have been an undoubted success, with the public already expressing their appreciation of the station and the amenities it affords them. The layout makes for simplicity' (though in an age before Health and Safety considerations, the necessity for passengers to cross the 'bus lanes to access the island' was disregarded). Suggestions were later made for traffic signals and bus shelters along the routes.

Among other more peaceful projects, the council repeatedly discussed the widening of Skerton Bridge, until in July the Minister of Transport authorised the project. On the outbreak of war, it was shelved indefinitely. The Mayor, Mrs H. L. Musgrave-Hoyle (only the second woman mayor of Lancaster) opened the new Ryelands Council School. In July the new Kingsway Baths were opened by the Minister of Health, Mr Walter Elliott, MP. Built at a cost of £59,000, they were reputedly 'the finest in the country', the frontage being 'a poem in stone'.

The Co-operative store's summer sale offered ladies' wear, including 'Millinery, Mantles and Hose, with silk hose at 1/- the pair'. Studholmes, Gorrills and Waring & Gillows also had sales in July, while the fast bowler Harold Larwood appeared at Lune Road for Blackpool. The Royal Lancashire Agricultural Show was held at Lancaster for the first time in fourteen years, but bad weather led to poor attendances, and eventually a loss of £2,000 was announced.

Political meetings continued to fuel opinion and prejudices. The prospective Liberal candidate, Colonel Ross, contended that recent crises had been the aftermath of Munich, and feared 'the immediate prospect, within five years, of a Fascist government under Mr Chamberlain. He must go'. Meanwhile the Women's Conservative and Unionist Association pledged their support for the Prime Minister. A Labour party rally was told that 'Fascism knows no peace, and Europe is drifting into war'. And in July, Mr Pat Sloan, editor of *Russia Today* told members of Lancaster's Left Book Club that if the public took action, they could force the government to sign a pact with the Soviet Union. 'There is a tremendous following for an alliance with Russia' he declared – only six weeks before the announcement of the Nazi–Soviet Pact, signed by foreign ministers Ribbentrop and Molotov.

Curiously there was a marked absence of such political meetings during the summer months, until, quite suddenly on 25 August the recall of parliament, following the announcement of the Molotov–Ribbentrop Pact, led the editor of the *Observer* to write 'there is an underlying anxiety as to what is to happen in the course of the next few days. There is a general desire that peace should be preserved – but not peace at any price'.

The last weekend of peace saw the Palladium screen Dorothy Lamour in *St Louis Blues,* and the Odeon *Love Affair* with Irene Dunne and Charles Boyer, but all LMS rail excursions were cancelled. 'This,' wrote the editor of the *Observer,* 'is the end of another week of anxiety, occasioned by the uncertainty of the international situation, with no relaxation of tension.' At the request of the Chief Constable, a poster asked, 'Your gas masks – are you prepared?'

The fateful announcement of the declaration of war was made in the edition of 8 September. Although the news was not unexpected, it nevertheless came as a blow.

Petrol rationing began on 18 September, with allocations from four to ten gallons a month (depending on horse-power), with two gallons for motor cycles. In anticipation of food rationing, households were required to register with grocers, and retailers had to apply for licences. Rationing of gas supplies would follow. A War Diary began to chronicle the events of the war, with the sinking of

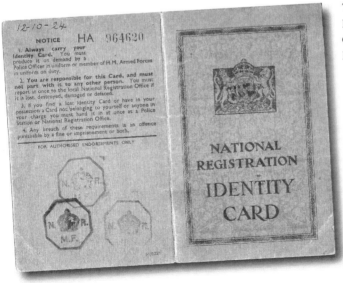

The National Registration Identity Card of Edmund Howard

the liner *Athenia* an early event, which city resident Mrs Townley survived. The diary soon disappeared from view. The cricket season ended early, and fixtures in the Ribblesdale Football League (in which Lancaster City played) were cancelled.

In November, a Comfort Fund for soldiers of the local regiment, the King's Own, was established. Knitted items – gloves, mittens, cap comforters, scarves, socks, jerseys and scarves were particularly requested. A National Savings campaign was led by the Mayor, and ration books and identity cards were distributed. Later instructions followed for the completion of the counterfoils to register with butchers for the meat ration. Although there is little information on men leaving to join the forces, shortage of staff is given as the reason for the reduction of the hours of opening of the General Post

Detail inside Edmund Howard's Identity Card, noting his changes of address

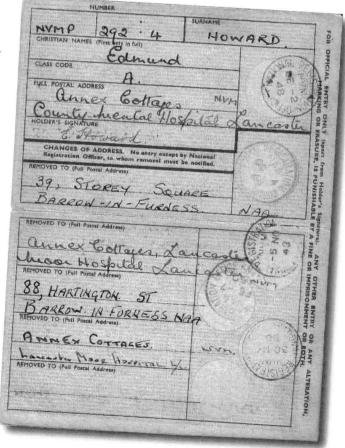

Office – now only open from 6.30 a.m. until 8.30 p.m., with only two deliveries of mail each day, at 7.45 a.m. and 3 p.m.

A Soldiers' Club in the Baptist Church Sunday School building in Robert Street provided canteen and library facilities, and was such a success that a similar club for women of the ATS was opened in neighbouring Sulyard Street Methodist Church hall.

CHAPTER 3

MILITARY SERVICE

Iɴ 1914, Britain had only a small professional army, and the first weeks of the war were filled with attempts to encourage volunteers – 3,000 men had responded by the end of the year. In 1939 the situation was different, though again a small regular army was backed by the Territorial Army (the author's father's TA battalion of the Royal Northumberland Fusiliers was mobilised in June, 1939). During 1939 attempts were made to encourage recruiting into the Territorial Army, local units of which were below strength. Lieutenant Colonel Oglethorpe of the firm of solicitors on Castle

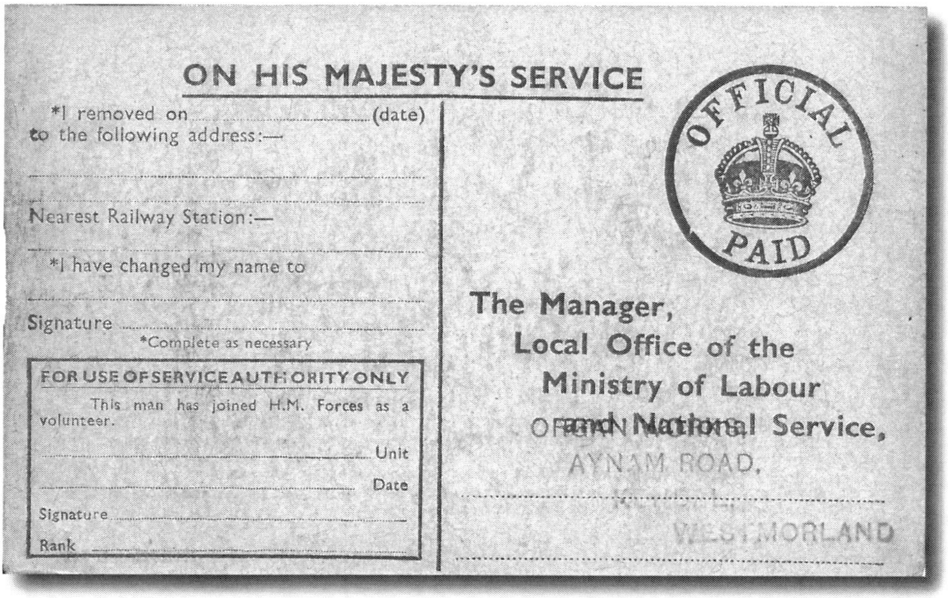

ON HIS MAJESTY'S SERVICE

*I removed on ....(date)
to the following address:—

Nearest Railway Station:—

*I have changed my name to

Signature ....
        *Complete as necessary

FOR USE OF SERVICE AUTHORITY ONLY
    This man has joined H.M. Forces as a volunteer.
.... Unit
.... Date
Signature...
Rank ....

OFFICIAL PAID

The Manager,
Local Office of the
Ministry of Labour
ofand National Service,
AYNAM ROAD,

WESTMORLAND

KEEP THIS CARD SAFELY

NATIONAL SERVICE ACTS, 1939-1941
Certificate of Registration

Occ. Classn. No. _025_   Registration No. BM. _8283._

Holder's Name _Howard   Edmund_

Home Address _Annex Cottages, County Mental Hospital_
Lancaster

Date of Birth _14 6 19.._

Holder's Signature _E. Howard_

READ THIS CAREFULLY

Care should be taken not to lose this Certificate, but in the event of loss, application for a duplicate should be made to the nearest office of the Ministry of Labour and National Service.

If you change your address, etc., you must complete the appropriate space on the other side of this certificate and post it at once. A new Certificate of Registration will then be sent to you.

If you voluntarily join H.M. Forces you should hand this certificate to the appropriate Service Officer. You should not voluntarily give up your employment because you have been registered for military service.

This certificate must be produced on request to a constable in uniform.

A person who uses or lends this certificate or allows it to be used by any other person with intent to deceive, renders himself liable to heavy penalties.

N.S.2.

*M10792 4/42 702

ATS at Quernmore Park

ATS pay parade at Ripley Hospital

Hill was appointed to command the fifth (TA) Battalion of the King's Own. In June the passage of the Military Service Act required registration of men of military age, with the first batches called up for six months' training, followed by three and a half years in the TA. To this Act, the Peace Pledge Union resolved 'this meeting expresses its strongest condemnation of the Government's Bill to conscript the youth of this country for training to kill their fellow-men'. There were a number of 'reserved occupations', including doctors and vets, teachers and engineers – 5 million in all, though they could volunteer for military service. Military age was at first defined as 20 to 41, later extended to begin at 18 and end at 51. The National Service Act of December 1941 compelled all unmarried women aged 20 to 30 to register for service in the auxiliary forces (Women's Royal Naval Service, Auxiliary Training Service or Women's Auxiliary Air Force), in Civil Defence, Women's Land Army or industry. A training unit of the ATS was established at Quernmore Park, and the Ripley Hospital was also commandeered for military training. Both men and women could apply for registration as conscientious objectors, their cases being heard by a tribunal.

Mr William Whalley of Alfred Street had, with his two brothers, served throughout the First World War. He announced in 1941 that he now had three sons in the armed forces – William, the eldest being an aircrew trainee with the Royal Air Force. The other two were in the army, Thomas in the King's Own, and Richard in the Border Regiment.

The *Guardian* began to publish a 'portrait gallery' of those serving – usually a panel of eight photographs.

ATS at Quernmore Park
(LG/LCM) COURTESY OF LANCASTER CITY MUSEUM PART OF LANCASHIRE MUSEUMS

CHAPTER 4

EVACUEES

IN January 1939, the Minister for Health, Mr Walter Elliot, MP, had announced that the government was making plans for evacuation from danger areas, and he directed all local authorities to determine whether they were vulnerable to aerial attack. The *Lancaster Observer* announced 'a new word has been coined – evacuees'. Later in the month the mayor presided over a meeting of billeting officers. Priority was to be given to children, who were to be kept in their school groups. Payments were to be made to householders of 10*s.* 6*d.* for one child and 8*s.* 6*d.* for each of two or more. Children under school age were to be accompanied by their mothers, with payments of 5*s.* per adult and 3*s.* per child. (In 1939 the author's mother, in rural Northumberland, had a mother from Bradford and her baby to stay – the two women remained in touch until in their 80s.)

Lancaster was thought to be safely out of the way of air raids, and so was designated as a 'reception area' – a safe place for children of Salford. Evacuation (Operation 'Pied Piper') began on Friday 1 September, with trains arriving every hour. 6,117 children with teachers and helpers arrived at the Castle Station, and were taken first to reception centres at Dallas Road and Skerton schools. (The city's elementary schools were closed while this operation proceeded, reopening several days later.) Householders were urged to receive children, and many did so.

A letter from the headmaster of Salford Grammar School

Evacuees at Greaves School, walking down Cheltenham Road
(LG/LCM) COURTESY OF LANCASTER CITY MUSEUM PART OF LANCASHIRE MUSEUMS

thanked the people of Lancaster for their 'wonderful reception. We have been deeply touched by the generosity and obvious friendliness of everyone.' Schools were evacuated en bloc, with Salford Grammar School sharing the premises of Lancaster Royal Grammar School, using its laboratories and sports facilities, with the rooms of the nearby Gregson Institute (then the parish hall of Christ Church) as classrooms. The Sedley Council School shared the premises of Greaves School, necessitating a shift system. A football league for the evacuated Salford schools was inaugurated, but many children returned home when there was no bombing, and by Christmas there were barely sufficient players to fulfil the fixtures. An appeal was made by the mayor for discarded clothing, both for children and for men – items should be taken to the Women's Voluntary Service in the St Anne's parish room in Friar Street.

Although it had been anticipated that bombing raids would begin at once, this did not happen, and within days, parents began to take their children home. By the end of the year only some 2,000 evacuees remained. In May 1940, the Queen sent letters of thanks to all who had made homes for evacuees, though by then further requests were being made by the council for offers of help, with a

Evacuees' Christmas party 1940
(LG/LCM) COURTESY OF LANCASTER CITY MUSEUM PART OF LANCASHIRE MUSEUMS

renewed evacuation foreseeable. The start of the German bombing campaign, universally known as 'the blitz', saw the return of numbers of evacuees, along the lines laid down at the outbreak of war. This led to poor relations with Salford Council, as Lancaster householders claimed that many of the children arrived poorly clad, poorly shod, and often unclean.

At a meeting of the WVS in July 1941, tributes were paid to 'the humble housewife' for the work of caring for these children. Problems over rationing were expressed, and there were suggestions that there could be central stocks of food, or the establishment of what Lord Woolton, Minister of Food, called 'British Restaurants' to provide meals. One was eventually opened in October 1942, 'to provide an amenity for workers unable to get to their homes for a normal midday meal'.

In 1944, the renewed air attacks on London by V1 'flying bombs' caused a new influx of evacuated mothers and children from the capital. A total of 1,341 were received between June and September. All had returned home a year later.

Emergency rations for evacuees being
distributed in County Street, September 1939
COURTESY OF LANCASHIRE COUNTY COUNCIL

Opening of British Restaurant in Church Street in 1942
(LG/LCM) COURTESY OF LANCASTER CITY MUSEUM PART OF LANCASHIRE MUSEUMS

CHAPTER 5

THE HOME GUARD AND THE ROYAL OBSERVER CORPS

T HE decision was taken in 1940 to create a body of Local Defence volunteers, mainly of old soldiers, who could take over some military duties. By July it was functioning in Lancaster, 'playing an important part in the scheme of national defence'. Mr Churchill later renamed the force the Home Guard. In September 1940, there was a church parade for the Lancaster detachment, led by the band of the King's Own, and commanded by Captain J. A. Black. The

editor of the *Observer* paid tribute to their smartness and their spirit, at the same time complimenting the ARP wardens, the Auxiliary Fire Service, the First Aid and Demolition squads. 'Their duties take them into danger zones where, without thought for their personal well-being, they go to the aid of their fellow-citizens'. There were four platoons, and a member of

A volunteer, with his previous military service indicated by his medal ribbons, poses in his newly issued battledress uniform, circa 1941.

DO A FRONT LINE JOB

YOU ARE URGENTLY NEEDED IN THE—

R.O.C

ROYAL OBSERVER CORPS

APPLY TO YOUR LOCAL CENTRE

An ROC recruiting poster

the platoon based at the Gregson Institute was interviewed as part of research for this book. Its Captain Mainwaring was the officer commanding the OTC contingent at LRGS, and it was tasked with the defence of the city from the east. Their secret weapon was a plank, with a roller skate under each end, and a short length of rope attached to each end. A group of the heroes would hide in the ditch at each side of Daisy Bank, and when the Panzer divisions rolled down the hill, would deploy the plank and puncture the tyres. When I asked my informant if he ever watched *Dad's Army* he replied, 'Whiles I do – but it were funnier than that'.

In the summer of 1941, the 3rd (City of Lancaster) Battalion, under the command of Colonel J. A. Black, was formally inspected on Giant Axe field, after which, led by the band of the King's Own, it paraded through the streets. There followed an exercise in the

OBSERVER CORPS

MODERN warfare's most dangerous weapon against life and property is the bomber, and the very essential job of preventing air raids is left to the Observer Corps.

In their various centres, every hour of the day and night, a shift of highly efficient and well-trained men, each with a telephone connected with three or four listening posts, study large-scale maps of the district divided into small squares. Another section is in contact by telephone with similar centres and also a sector of the Fighter Command.

Each time a 'plane is sighted at one of the listening posts, a report is sent to the centre and small counters are laid on the map plotting the course of the machine. Other men, seeing the counters, report the map number of each of them to the appropriate authority. Thus the machinery of air defence is kept moving and the presence of hostile or unidentified aircraft is made known instantly to those who direct operations of anti-aircraft guns, searchlights and fighter 'planes.

The listening posts are manned by people who are trained to pick out a 'plane on sight, to know whether they are friendly or hostile, and also to follow their course even if they are invisible.

Their training includes the collation of information in such a way that, should it be necessary, defence measures may be put into operation at a moment's notice. All the men, who are now under the jurisdiction of the Air Ministry, do their observation work in many cases without giving up their ordinary work. They are liable for duty at any time, and often sleep at the centre. They work with remarkable concentration and efficiency, and are all responsible and intelligent men who may be depended upon to stand up to the strain without losing their mental agility or ability to make decisions.

That this organisation could be brought to its present state of high efficiency is a tribute to its staff and those who have trained it and control it.

Air raid precautions, First Observer Corps control room at the castle, October 1939.
COURTESY OF LANCASHIRE COUNTY COUNCIL

Carnforth area, in which three of the platoons captured a bridge, held by the other platoon. At first their only weapons had been the First World War Lee–Enfield .303 rifles from the armoury of the Officers' Training Corps at the Royal Grammar School (the older cadets had wanted to join, but were ruled to be too young), but by now the unit was equipped with modern weapons, including machine guns, and had good wireless communications. A week-long recruiting campaign was held in the following year, and weekend tented training camps were held.

In 1944 Lieutenant-Colonel J. A. Black, who had commanded

the Lancaster battalion since its formation was transferred to staff duties over a wider area, and Major F. E. Winwell, his deputy for the past four years, took over. At the end of the year, the Home Guard was 'stood down', there being no conceivable possibility of an invasion.

The creation of the Observer Corps predated that of the Home Guard: it dates from 1925, when it was realised that any future war would involve aerial attack. With a motto 'Forewarned is Forearmed', its members were rated as special constables, though many of them retained a first war military rank. The Lancaster unit was formed in 1938, and was initially housed in an upper room in Hadrian's Tower in Lancaster Castle. This proved damp and inconvenient of access, and the basement of the then District Bank (now the NatWest Bank) in Church Street became its new control room. It was designated 29 (Lancaster) Group, later merging with 32 (Carlisle)Group, to form North West Area. Its first Controller was Mr H. Cross, soon succeeded by Lieutenant Colonel L. I. Cowper (ex King's Own) who became the Observer Group Commandant. There were four crews, A, B, C and D, who operated in rota. With sandbagged rooftop posts and a telephone, long cold vigils were kept. From 1939 RDF (Radio Direction Finding, later known as radar) gave early warning, with the observers taking over once the raiders had reached land. For its part in the Battle of Britain, the corps was given its royal title in 1941, and women were admitted in the same year. It now had a blue battledress uniform, and a badge depicting an Elizabethan at an armada year beacon. Aircraft recognition training was of prime importance, and competitions were regularly held. The Corps was stood down in May 1945, but revived two years later, and was active throughout the Cold War.

A.F.S. in training, Chief Inspector Walker was responsible for the training, several practices in full dress were held in the gas works yard.

COURTESY OF LANCASHIRE COUNTY COUNCIL

CHAPTER 6

AIR RAID PRECAUTIONS

THE bombing raids by Zeppelin airships and Gotha aircraft in the First World War had led to the formation of a government Air Raid Precautions Committee in 1924, and an ARP Act of January 1938 compelled local authorities to appoint ARP Wardens (volunteers) and to establish emergency services – ambulances, first aid posts and rescue, repair and demolition squads. A volunteer Auxiliary Fire Service was inaugurated.

From the beginning of 1939, government directives on air raid precautions had begun to arrive. Based on observations of events in the Spanish civil war, the assumption was that 'the bomber will always get through'. Councillor V. H. Cross advocated the building of bomb-proof shelters in each street, with an underground control centre in Dalton Square.

Black-out practices were held, not only to check on the efficiency of the black-out, but also of the emergency services, 'incidents' being staged to involve the fire services, police, first aid and repair groups. As soon as war was declared, lighting restrictions on buildings and vehicles, and the carrying of gas masks were implemented – gas attacks were also greatly feared. 41,000 adult gas masks, and helmets for children under two years, were issued, with a supply of masks for children from two to four made in early 1940. By then, with no raids having occurred, it was apparent that few people were carrying their masks. There was an immediate closure of cinemas and theatres, but later, to raise morale, these reopened with the government

Gas attack exercise outside 1, King Street, Lancaster

encouraging people to attend performances. The Lord Lieutenant, the Earl of Derby, visited the ARP centre and congratulated the volunteer staff on their whole-hearted spirit of co-operation. However, despite the enrolment of 283 ARP personnel, only 153 responded when an exercise was held.

There followed a spate of minor accidents in the blackout conditions, with the first fatality being the death of 61-year-old Mr Ernest Watson of Dorrington Road, killed by a car in Thurnham Street. There was not to be a similar accident until 1944, when a woman was knocked down in Dalton Square in the early morning by a corporation refuse collection vehicle. In both cases the coroner recorded a verdict of accidental death.

Testing of the air raid warning sirens was advertised for 15 December 1939, and again on 18 January 1940. The public was warned that the signals would be first a steady note for two minutes, as a general warning, followed after another two minutes by an intermittent signal as the alert for a raid. Another steady note would indicate that the danger had passed. It was found that the signals could not easily be heard in workshops where heavy machinery was being operated. By the middle of 1940 a series of basement shelters in hotels and the old Town Hall had been established, together with trenches in parks and other places. As air raids increased in the autumn of 1940, there was increasing demand for brick-built street shelters, the matter coming before several council meetings. The firm Dilworths, which had already converted basement shelters in four locations, now had a tender for £187 18s. 7d. for the construction of four surface shelters accepted, and tenders were invited for others on the Newton estate. Eventually the building of 175 was planned. These were single brick, rectangular boxes, with a concrete lid and offered rather dubious security. The author recalls air raid practices at school, in which pupils were led into the shelters to sit on the wooden benches until the raid was assumed to have passed. Gas masks did give some protection from the stench of the two chemical toilets in cubicles screened by hessian sheets. Anderson shelters were issued to those householders with gardens.

In 1941 it was discovered that shelters built (to the County Council specifications) with lime mortar were unsafe, and thirty had to be demolished, slowing down the work even more. Reports were made of vandalism in the shelters, especially the smashing of lampshades and the theft of bulbs. This was put down to the juvenile crime, about which the Chief Constable, magistrates and the newspapers made regular complaints. The absence of fathers, the opportunities afforded by the blackout, and the unsettling nature of the war were all blamed. There was also damage to the corporation omnibuses to which, it was claimed, members of the public, 'turned a blind eye'.

The ARP Committee was renamed the Civil Defence Committee, and its wardens were issued with the blue battledress and greatcoat of the Civil Defence workers. One of the first announcements of the new committee was that there was no prospect of the complete provision of shelters in the next two years. From June, all men from 16 to 60 were required to register at the Employment exchange for Civil Defence duties. For householders, Gillows offered blackout material, and brown gummed tape for windows (to prevent flying glass) while Manserghs went one better by offering to make up their material into curtains, free of charge. Calvert & Heald could provide 'anti-splinter adhesive net' as well as a galvanised sand box with scoop and hoe (26s.). They expected a small consignment of stirrup pumps to retail at £1: 'place your order now'.

The ladies' outfitters Studholmes offered 'air raid siren suits for ladies and children, from 25s. 9d., in cosy and warm wool velour' as well as 'slacks – very useful for ARP duties'. (The wearing of slacks, or trousers, by ladies had been considered somewhat daring.)

The magnificent medieval choir stalls from the Priory Church were taken to an undisclosed place of safety.

From October 1941 there were test gas attacks in the city centre,

Removing Choir stalls from Lancaster Priory Church
(LG/LCM) COURTESY OF LANCASTER CITY MUSEUM PART OF LANCASHIRE MUSEUMS

using tear gas. People were forewarned of these, but even so there were those who did not carry gas masks, and so suffered from itchy eyes. The Home Guard and Civil Defence workers were involved, and motorists and cyclists found that the masks proved no hindrance.

In 1942, 1,000 indoor Morrison shelters were received, but there were only 100 requests for their issue in the first month. It appeared that, as with the failure to carry gas masks, the absence of air raids in the locality had led to complacency. A report on the severe damage caused by a 'Baedeker Raid' on Exeter (thought to be in a safe area) was used as a warning that this could happen to Lancaster. In practice, it appears that the complacency was justified, as there never was an air raid on Lancaster. One bomb – probably jettisoned by a German bomber en route to the docks at Barrow-in-Furness, fell on a house in Ulster Road, Bowerham. It was the end house of a terrace, looking onto a ginnel, and for years afterwards its surviving neighbour had an incongruous brick end wall (the nineteenth-century houses were stone-built) while the site was a builder's yard. It is only a few years since the house was rebuilt in a replica form.

CHAPTER 7

THE 'PHONEY WAR' ENDS

As usual the new year was heralded by January sales in the local shops, and by a variety of entertainments. These included, at the Palladium, Gracie Fields in *Shipyard Sally*, and Lupino Lane in *Lambeth Walk* at the Odeon. The Palace screened Johnny Weissmuller and Maureen O'Hara in *Tarzan Finds a Son*, while the pantomime was *Mother Goose*. A New Year party for the remaining evacuees was a great success, leading to a suggestion by the editor of the *Observer* that the similar event for the elderly (provided by the generosity of the late Mr Herbert Storey) be revived.

A speech by Lord Hankey in the House of Lords was quoted – speaking of economic warfare and the blockade, he asserted optimistically that 'Germany is feeling the pinch – the conditions of life there are strained'. People were advised 'not to listen to Lord Haw Haw, the expatriate Englishman William Joyce who broadcast speeches designed to spread alarm and undermine morale.'

An appeal was made for the salvage of waste materials – paper, metal, rags and bottles. Some 5,000 tons of waste paper was needed by industry every month, and only 1,000 tons was being collected. A temporary shortage of coal for domestic use was announced.

Rationing of foods began in January 1940, with bacon (4 ounces per week), sugar (12 ounces) and butter (4 ounces) the first items. In March 1941, meat rationing began. Each adult was entitled to meat to the value of 1*s*. 10*d*. per week (11*d*. for a child). Householders could

Salvage collection in Middle Street, 1940
(LG/LCM) COURTESY OF LANCASTER CITY MUSEUM PART OF LANCASHIRE MUSEUMS

choose a larger amount of the cheaper cuts, while offal, poultry and game were not rationed. The author recollects the local poulterer with chickens and rabbits strung up outside his shop. Cheese was rationed at one ounce per week from May 1941, and, after a brief rise to 8 ounces, went back to 3 ounces in 1943. Jam, marmalade, syrup or treacle were rationed at 8 ounces per month. In July 1940 cheap milk (at 2*d.* per pint) was made available to expectant and nursing mothers, and to children under five. For those on low incomes (40 shillings a week for a couple, or 27s. 6*d.* for single mothers, or the unemployed) the milk was free. The initial response, however, was disappointing. A government 'Dig for Victory' campaign, urging civilians to grow vegetables also brought a poor initial response. Although each person was entitled to an egg a week, 'shell eggs', as they became known, were often unobtainable, and dried egg substitute was offered – it was suitable only for scrambled egg or omelettes.

At this time there was great controversy over the proposed opening of cinemas on Sundays. This had long been permitted in Morecambe, but the Watch Committee in Lancaster had always set its face against the practice. There was division of opinion both on the council, and among the public, while the Anglican and Free Churches were in opposition. Eventually the proposal was carried by 18 votes to 12 on the council (the mayor leading the opposition), and the first licences were issued in September 1940.

Tribunals for the consideration of the claims of conscientious objectors were held in the Civil Court in the castle. Seventeen applications from the district (though none from the city was heard at the first session. Of these five were registered, ten rejected (though these were listed as liable to call-up only for non-combatant duties) and two applications were withdrawn.

Severe criticism of the Prime Minister and of his National Government was again made by Lieutenant Colonel Ross, prospective Liberal Candidate. He had been quiet since the outbreak of war, but now attacked Mr Chamberlain's 'lack of initiative'. He claimed that members of his government only paid 'a lip-service to democracy' and that it showed 'a tendency to develop a fascist state'.

A sunny Easter made for a very successful William Smith Festival on Giant Axe, with the Boys' National School and the Cathedral School winning the senior and junior football trophies. The German invasion of Norway brought to an end the import of wood pulp for paper making (already difficult), and led to a naval campaign in which both sides suffered severe losses.

In May the king and queen paid a visit to the city. For security reasons there had been no advance publicity, but rumours had begun to spread a day or two in advance. The mayor and other prominent citizens were presented, before their majesties visited Bowerham

Cutting railings at Williamson Park

Barracks. Here 800 soldiers were drawn up, the queen inspecting the women of the ATS detachment before talking to a group of wounded personnel.

The local press had adopted a 'business as usual' attitude so far with only matters of evacuation, air raid precautions and rationing having much mention. Now, however, the German invasion of Denmark and Norway led to the cry 'Who is next ?' – swiftly answered by the invasion first of the Low Countries and then of France. 'We are fighting for our very existence' exclaimed the editor of the *Observer*.

Regular cookery lessons were given at the Gas Board's showrooms in Market Square. At one the recipes demonstrated included carrot marmalade, carrot chutney and bean cutlets. There was a glut of carrots, and it was put about that these improved the night vision of the bomber crews, with the result that aircrew were fed carrots at every meal. (This information came from one of the author's RAF flying instructors.)

'These are serious days', declared an editorial, 'our position as a nation has never been more critical than it is now. We are engaged, with our allies, in a life and death struggle with an enemy whose tactics are ruthless'. Rumours of heavy losses among 'local lads' proliferated, and attacks from the air were seen as a real possibility. Emergency water supply tanks each containing 5,000 gallons of fresh water were set up at various points, and there were increasing prosecutions for neglecting the blackout regulations. The long hot summer of 1940 brought drought, with repeated official demands for economy of water, combined with warnings that supplies might be cut off. Rainfall in the autumn eased matters, but the public was warned that economy still had to be observed, and the ban on washing windows, flagstones, and cars remained, under threat of prosecution. The response to the national savings drive was good, with £20,000 raised in four weeks, but the initial appeal for waste paper salvage was poor. After repeated demands, it improved greatly.

The Editor of FOOD FACTS *invites you to*

Meet your New

RATION BOOK

For a whole year of meals your ration book will be your food-friend and provider. It's high time you got acquainted — so let's effect an introduction! Five minutes is all it will take. Better attend to it now — but if you haven't your ration book handy, *cut this out and go through it as soon as you can.*

GENERAL BOOK (buff)
and JUNIOR BOOK (blue)

THE FRONT COVER (p. 1). See that the entries are correct and agree with those on your identity card.

PAGES 2, 3, 4. You needn't trouble with these yet awhile.

CLOTHING BOOK. Now comes a separate section for the clothing book. It has pink covers. Its pages are numbered at the foot I to VII and stapled together. Hold the book in your left hand (you'll find it most convenient to turn it upside down) and cut out the whole clothing book where a cutting-line is marked. Fill in your name, address and National Registration number on the first pink page; and there you have your clothing book ready for use on September 1st.

PAGES 5 - 8. *All* the foods you are registered for are now grouped together on a page: a little rearrangement which will save a lot of time in the cancelling of the coupons by the shops.

The sugar spaces have small subdivisions marked P, Q, R, S. Here P is for preserves: Q, R and S won't be used at present.

PAGES 9, 10. The top coupons are for tea. Four will be *cut out* for each ration period, as now. These coupons are printed back and front to make sorting easier for the shopkeeper: don't be misled into thinking they give you a double ration! The coupons marked "K" are spare ones. Do nothing with them.

PAGES 11, 12. More spares.

PAGES 13 - 24. These are the points pages — no change here.

PAGES 25-32. These are your *personal* points coupons, printed in the book this time instead of on a separate sheet. If you want to use them without the ration book you can cut out a page at a time but you must fill in your name and National Registration number at the top of each page you cut out. *Do not cut out a page until you need to use it.* The first page lasts to October 16th.

PAGES 33, 34. T...

Page 35. You must fill in section A before the book can be used — your name, address and National Registration number, the number of your new Ration Book (copied from the sideways printing at the bottom right-hand corner of the front cover) and if you are under 18, your date of birth.

PAGE 36. Write your present retailers' names and addresses in the spaces provided.

PAGE 37. If you deposit points or tea coupons, this is where you write the name and address of the retailer, and he initials the entry.

BACK COVER (p. 38) is divided into two main panels. Panel 1 (on the left) is for soap. Panel 2 won't be used yet.

Depositing of pages.

You can, if you and the retailer wish, deposit any sections of pages 5 and 7 with a retailer, but you must complete the side panels and get the retailer to enter "D" in the panel against his name on page 36.

The half-page tea coupons or sections of points coupons may also be deposited with a retailer provided that your name and National Registration number are entered on them and you make the entries on page 37 and get the retailer to initial them.

Registration with Retailers.

This time you do not have to re-register but if you want to change a retailer you may do so by applying to the Food Office between Aug. 8th and 28th. You cannot change your milk retailer.

Special Cheese Ration.

If you have been granted a special cheese ration you can continue to receive it until August 21st. If you wish to renew this apply to the Food Office before that date.

CHILD'S BOOK (green)

The only differences are that one meat coupon is available per week instead of two, coupons "O" on page 9 will be used when you buy oranges, and pages are provided at the back of the book for vitamins

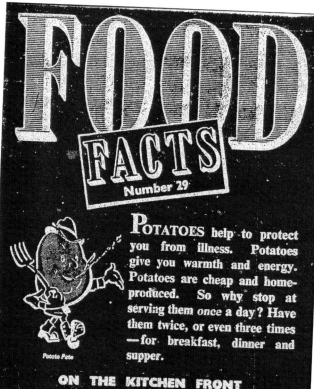

FOOD FACTS
Number 29

POTATOES help to protect you from illness. Potatoes give you warmth and energy. Potatoes are cheap and home-produced. So why stop at serving them once a day? Have them twice, or even three times — for breakfast, dinner and supper.

Potato Pete

ON THE KITCHEN FRONT

Coffee Potato Scones

Sift 6 ozs. plain flour, 2 level teaspoonfuls baking powder and ½ teaspoonful salt in a basin. Mix thoroughly with 4 ozs. mashed potato. Rub in 2 ozs. fat with the tips of the fingers. Blend to a soft dough with ¼ teacupful strong, milky, sweetened coffee. Roll out to ¼ inch thickness on a floured board and cut into rounds. Glaze the tops with a little milk. Bake on greased baking sheets in a hot oven for 15 minutes.

Potato Drop Scones

Rub 2 ozs. mashed potato into 4 ozs. flour already salted with ¼ teaspoonful salt. Make into a stiff batter with ½ a beaten egg and 1 gill milk. Allow to stand for a time. Sift in a small teaspoonful cream of tartar, a small level teaspoonful bicarbonate of soda and ½ oz. sugar just before cooking. Cook in spoonfuls — as for Scotch drop scones — on a greased girdle or in a heavy frying-pan. Serve with a little hot jam.

Surprise Potato Balls

Cook 1 lb. potatoes and beat well with a fork. Add a large grated carrot, 1 teaspoonful chopped parsley and some salt and pepper. Use a little milk, if necessary, to bind the mixture, but do not make it wet. Form into balls. Make a hole in each, drop in a small teaspoonful of sweet pickle and close the hole. Roll the balls in browned breadcrumbs, place on a greased baking sheet. Bake in a moderate oven for 15 to 20 minutes.

These are good for any and every meal.

Parsley Potato Cakes

Here is a new breakfast dish which you can prepare the day before.

Boil 1 lb. potatoes and mash them while hot with a very little hot milk. Season with salt and pepper to taste.

Next morning, add a tablespoonful chopped parsley. Shape the mixture into little cakes, cover well with browned breadcrumbs and pan fry in a little hot fat, or bake in the oven.

FOOD FACTS

Number 27

THAN IKS to the hard work of our farmers and growers, there are fine supplies of potatoes, carrots and oatmeal in the Country. Three foods giving energy and protection against illness — let us eat some of each every day.

NB

The crews of our mine-sweepers are always risking their lives to bring you food, so don't waste any. You wouldn't if you'd done any sweeping yourself!

ON THE KITCHEN FRONT

Potato Carrot Pancake

Well-seasoned mashed potato combined with cooked carrot makes a wholesome and savoury-tasting pancake. Whip the mashed potato to a loose creamy consistency. Season well with pepper and salt and add some diced cooked carrot. Pan-fried slowly in a very little fat it develops a deliciously crisp crust, but it can be baked to a good brown in the oven if preferred.

Potato Basket

Scrub 1 lb. potatoes and boil gently in a very little water. When they are nearly cooked, drain off the liquid reserving it for stock. Let them finish cooking in their own steam by covering them closely with a folded cloth under the lid and

You can hear all kinds of food tips on the wireless at 8.15 every morning

minutes, and mix them with a sauce made from 1 oz. dripping, 1 oz. oatmeal and ½ pint milk or stock, and salt and pepper to taste. When the potato basket is cooked, turn it out and fill it with the hot carrot mixture. Heat in the oven for a few minutes and serve piping hot. (*Enough for four.*)

Oatmeal Stuffing

This is particularly useful for making meat, fish or poultry go further.

Boil 3 ozs. coarse oatmeal in 1¼ teacupfuls water for 30 minutes. Mix well with 2 ozs. breadcrumbs, salt and pepper, 1 teaspoonful mixed sweet herbs, 1 teaspoonful chopped parsley, 1 grated onion (if you can get it) and a pinch of mace if liked. Bind with a little melted dripping if necessary.

When M. Reynaud had resigned as prime minister of France, he was replaced by Marshal Petain, hero of the defence of Verdun in 1916. The optimism which greeted this news was soon shattered when his first action was to ask for peace terms. The collapse of France meant that this country, with the Empire, now stood alone, but there was no doubt that we should continue the struggle.

The evacuation of some 330,000 troops from Dunkirk gave some measure of hope, but the prime minister was quick to warn against making too much of this. Though it was 'a miracle of deliverance', we had suffered 'a colossal military disaster. Wars are not won by evacuations'. There was understandable anxiety about casualties to 'local lads', but solid news (as opposed to widespread rumours) was slow to emerge. Eventually it was confirmed that of 5 King's Own, Major A. Barton, Captains R. E. Gregory, R. E. Smalley and G. E. Middleton (son of the Town Clerk), Lieutenant G. Airey, CSM Frank Knight and all four brothers of the Howe family of Hubert Street were safe. The first known casualty was Captain H. C. Coulson, but the OBE (military division) was awarded to Major R. M. J. Goldie and the Military Cross to Second Lieutenant F. R. Richardson, an Old Lancastrian.

At this point, Lord Beaverbrook, Minister of Aircraft Production, made his celebrated appeal for scrap – 'Pots and pans make planes'. Housewives were encouraged to give not only pots and pans, but also kettles, vacuum cleaners, hat pegs, hangers, bathroom fittings and household ornaments to WVS centres. It is by no means clear how far any of these would help to build 'Hurricanes, Blenheims or Wellingtons': the impact probably was on morale. The removal of old, First World War artillery pieces from beside the Shire Court for scrap probably had more effect. Equally, the removal of iron railings from outside houses and from Williamson Park was likely to have been of dubious value.

The decision to remove signposts to confuse an invader probably caused more confusion to ordinary travellers, but the arrest of two local members of the British Union of Fascists for issuing propaganda was greeted with satisfaction. There was an appeal for labour to help build defence works, designed to hamper the enemy. The concrete 'pill-box' emplacements largely survive, though their efficacy must be in doubt. Local examples include the very rational one covering the railway line north of Carnforth station, but one queries the need for a box covering the Lune bridge near Gressingham. A huge amount of material, as well as labour must have been expended.

The expansion of the war now reached south-east Europe, with Soviet Russia's demands for Bessarabia and the northern Bukovina to be ceded by Rumania. (Russia had already invaded Finland in the 'Winter War' of 1939 and had been expelled from the League of Nations as a result.) Japan joined the Axis powers, though was not yet belligerent.

The August Bank Holiday (then held on the first Monday of the month) was cancelled, on the grounds that 'there must be no slackening of the war effort – production of the sinews of war must continue unabated'. There had been a good deal of publicity to national savings schemes with exhortations such as 'Thrift will help this nation to win the war – now is the time to save'. Then, in November 1940 came War Weapons Week, a massive national drive which in Lancaster aimed to raise £300,000 (of which £75,000 was to re-equip the destroyer HMS *Lancaster* (see Chapter 11). Parades were held to generate a huge response, with £389,000 raised inside two weeks.

CHAPTER 8

CASUALTIES

THE first casualty of the war was Engine Room Artificer J. C. Mockett of Caton Road. After leaving LRGS, he had followed an engineering apprenticeship and had joined the Royal Navy in 1934. He lost his life in the submarine HMS *Oxley* on 10 September 1939, leaving a widow and two young children. The next was the death of OL Pilot Officer J. Musgrave, killed when his Whitley bomber crashed on a training flight in Oxfordshire. His father, a Squadron Leader, donated a handsome silver trophy to the School in his memory.

At Dunkirk, Lieutenant G. Chippendale of the Royal Engineers was taken off the beaches aboard the Royal Navy destroyer HMS *Grafton* but lost his life when the ship was hit by a torpedo fired by U62. Sinking in shallow water, most of those on board were taken off, and only three men apart from Lieutenant Chippendale lost their lives.

In February 1941, the death of Sergeant Pilot Oliver Cousins of Hala Carr farm was recorded. He was killed in what must have been a training flight in Scotland and his funeral, at St Paul's Church, Scotforth was attended by large numbers of the farming community. He was buried with full military honours in Scotforth cemetery. Later in the year the funeral was held at St Peter's Cathedral of aircrew Sergeant Thomas Highton DFM, of Langdale Road and a former pupil of the Cathedral School, whose pupils lined East

Road as the cortege moved, with RAF Guard of Honour, to the city cemetery.

Throughout the war, information about casualties had been sketchy. In the First World War, week by week, casualties were identified in both local newspapers by name, rank and unit, with a photograph, address and details of family. In the Second World War, there was little military activity at first. Although the British Expeditionary Force had been deployed in France on the outbreak of war, it saw no action for the period of the 'phoney war' until the German invasion of the Low Countries and France, and then only for the few weeks until the evacuation from Dunkirk. Thereafter (apart from the, largely Canadian, raid on Dieppe) there was no military action in north-west Europe until 1944. The Eighth army in north Africa and the Fourteenth army in the far east were involved in fighting as were the Royal Navy and Royal Air Force. Of the 118 former pupils of LRGS who died, no fewer than sixty are simply described as 'missing on air operations, believed dead'. In 1940 the Royal Artillery did give information about several of its members. Three local men, posted as missing at Dunkirk, were revealed to be prisoners of war. They were Gunner Peter Rack of 4, Newlands Avenue, a driver, Gunner Alec Parker of Eden Park, and Sergeant Bennett, son of Mr T. Bennett, a bookbinder with a business in Frances Passage. RASC soldier C. S. Rogers of Slyne Road was also listed as a prisoner of war in 1941, while the following year group photographs of PoWs were published, identifying Gunners (Royal Artillery) G. Atkinson of Prospect Street, E. Rigg and A. Hodgson of the Marsh, and Pte L. Etherington (King's Own) of Ridge Street. In the Far East, Gunner R. Carney of Bath Street was missing in Malaya (he was later found to be a prisoner of the Japanese), and Boy (First Class) G. Brakewell of Dale Street was missing, believed killed. He had served in the cruiser HMS *Exeter*, which was sunk in the battle of the Java Sea in 1942, though this loss was not announced at the time.

Others discovered to be PoWs in Italy included Stoker James Lambert of Coverdale Road, Sergeant E. W. Scott (RASC) and Fred Crabtree of Noel Road while Captain J. G. Swainson of the law practice on Castle Hill had been captured by the Japanese in Singapore. Others held prisoner by the Japanese included Lieutenant Colonel G. E. C. Rossall (OL) of the RASC, taken in Singapore, Sergeant W. Bowker, taken in Malaya and Aircraftman R. F. Elleray of Meeting House Lane (also captured in Singapore). Lance Bombardier K. Dowbiggin of Thornfield, serving with the Royal Field Artillery was also in Japanese hands. A former pupil of the Friends School, he had been manager for the Footlights Club. Increasingly, during 1943, there were reports of others in Japanese hands. Most of these had been captured in the early Japanese offensives, but the names were only now released. They included Gunner C. D. Reay, Royal Artillery, of The Forge, Scotforth, Sergeant F. D. King of Summersgill Road (REME) and Sergeant W. Potter, all taken at Singapore.

Sergeant (Air Gunner) H. Wilcock, of Vicarage Lane and formerly of the Boys' National School lost his life when his Wellington bomber was shot down, and others reported lost included Flying Officers E. Lambert and J. C. Smith, Second Lieutenant W. A. Smith and Lieutenant W. Hind of the Royal Engineers, who had achieved first class honours at Downing College Cambridge. Flight Sergeant J. Creighton of Barton Road was killed in action He and his brother, Sergeant R. Creighton, killed the previous year, are commemorated by a mathematics prize at their old school, LRGS. Pilot Officer C. Halliday of Queen Street was posted as missing in action after a raid on Cologne. Lieutenant J. H. Dean of Wingate Saul Road was serving with a bomb disposal unit of the Royal Engineers, and lost his life while removing the detonator of a German bomb. In 1944 the death was announced of a former Lancaster CC cricketer, Major C. G. Ford of the Grenadier Guards. Also a member of the Footlights Club, he had taken the roe of Sir Percy Blakeney in their pre-war production of *The Scarlet Pimpernel*.

The posthumous award of Lloyds War medal was announced to Wireless Operator G. Barker of the Merchant Navy, an Old Lancastrian. While his ship was under fire from a German submarine, he continued to send out a signal, giving the position, with the result that his shipmates were picked up by a British warship which had picked up the message.

Stoker John Atkinson of 108 Prospect Street was posted as 'missing presumed dead', after the loss of the destroyer HMS *Diamond* in the evacuation of Crete, but Writer Keith Thomas cabled his parents to say that he was safe. He had been serving in HMS *Ark Royal*, sunk on 4 November 1941 (again, this loss was not made public). RSM R. A. Parker of Greenfield Street, who had been serving with the RAMC in the Middle East, was confirmed as a PoW, as were Gunner G. Turner of Stodday, captured at Dunkirk, and Sergeant E. M. Croft of 9, Railway Street, serving with the RASC. Corporal G. Cruikshank of Newsham Road, an armourer with the RAF, was killed in an air raid on Malta, and Sergeant (Flight Engineer) K. Watson, a former pupil of the Boys' National School was posted as missing after a raid on Hamburg. The air assault on Germany was defended, as retaliation for German raids on this country.

In the same week in July 1943, the parents of two brothers from Langdale Road learnt that AB Albert Bettany of the Royal Navy had lost his life, and Desmond was a prisoner in Japanese hands, as were Gunner W. Houghton of Skiddaw Road and Trooper W. Liver of Pinfold Lane.

Home from Italy came Driver W. Morgan of the Royal Horse Artillery. He had been captured by the German Afrika Korps at the battle of Gazala in Libya (as was the author's father) and sent to a PoW camp in Italy. He took advantage of the confusion attendant on that country's capitulation in September 1943 to escape and make his way south to the advancing British troops. He was fortunate, having no identification, that there were three soldiers there who recognised him. (My father, a prisoner in a northern camp, escaped and eventually managed to reach Switzerland.)

CHAPTER 9

DECORATIONS

THE Military Cross was awarded to four army officers. These were – Second Lieutenant C. U. J. Kay-Shuttleworth, Major H. Houghton of the Royal Artillery (service in the Middle East), Major D. Morris (Royal Horse Artillery) of Haverbreaks Place – service in North Africa, Major R. Morris (Royal Armoured Corps) – service in Burma, and to the Reverend R. H. Gaydon, minister at Lancaster Baptist Church, serving as Chaplain with the Royal Air Force in the Middle East.

The Distinguished Flying Cross was awarded to seven aircrew officers of the Royal Air Force. They were Pilot Officers T. L. Rushton and D. Langton, Flying Officers A. Winskill, C. W. Shires and M. Elliott and Warrant Officer J. H. Bushby, while Pilot Officer T. H. Baker won a DFC to add to the DFM he had earlier won as a Sergeant pilot. He was later shot down and spent the rest of the war as a prisoner. Other Distinguished Flying Medals were won by aircrew NCOs, Flight Sergeant navigator H. Bibby and Sergeants H. J. King, T. Highton and O. H. Shufflebottom.

A Distinguished Conduct Medal was awarded to Private D. Brown of the King's Own, while there were twelve winners of the Military Medal. They were Guardsman D. Clarke (in Italy), Trooper J. Whitbread with the Royal Tank Regiment in North Africa, Fusilier H. Pattinson (Lancashire Fusiliers), Lance Corporal C. Champion of Gerrard Street (with the Border Regiment in Burma 1944), Lance

Bombardiers J. H. Threlfall (RA)and A. Lingwood (RA) in Italy, Corporals G. Wilson (Royal Armoured Corps) and G. S. Pennington in north-west Europe 1944, W. L. Wilson with 13/18 Hussars on D-Day, and W. D. Scriven of the Durham Light Infantry, Sergeants T. Lyth with the Royal Irish Fusiliers in Italy, and R. E. Little (Royal Armoured Corps) in Normandy. The Navy's Distinguished Service Medal was awarded to Signalman F. J. Bradshaw.

British Empire Medals went to Petty Officer J. Rudd, with Combined Operations, to Flight Sergeant J. Thompson (RAF ground crew), to Private J. Glover of the Royal Army Medical Corps for heroism when his hospital ship, bound for Malta was bombed, and to Chief Petty Officer L. Todd, for work in mine disposal. (He had been mentioned in dispatches while serving in HMS *Arethusa* at the battle of Dogger Bank in 1915.) VAD Corporal E. M. Stewart was also awarded the BEM for her work as a nurse at Lancaster Military Hospital. The MBE (Military Division) was awarded to RSM M. Walsh of the Royal Field Artillery.

Finally, the Croix de Guerre was awarded by the Free French government to Lancaster's Member of Parliament Captain F. H. McLean. As a liaison officer he had flown with their parachute regiment in the Near East, on all their operations. He reached the rank of Brigadier by the end of the war.

CHAPTER 10

LANCASTER SCHOOLS

B**Y** far the oldest school in Lancaster (and, indeed in the county) was the Royal Grammar School. Originating in about 1235, it had been endowed by John Gardyner, thrice Mayor of Lancaster, by 1472, and was given its royal title by Queen Victoria in 1851. In January 1939, the appointment as Headmaster of Mr R. R. Timberlake was announced, to take effect from Easter. Like his predecessor, Dr J. H. Shackleton-Bailey (now vicar of St Michael's-on-Wyre), he was taking over on the eve of a world war, with particular problems for a school with boarders. At the Speech Day of October 1940, he referred to members of staff and former pupils (at least 220 already) who were serving in the armed forces. By 1944, the total was over 1,000. Although so many of the school's former pupils saw service in the Second World War, finding their details has been difficult. From 1914 to 1918 the editor of the termly magazine recorded those serving, those enlisting, promotions, decorations, wounds and deaths. His successor from 1939 to 1945 simply listed those enlisting, often without more detail than 'army' or 'Royal Navy'. A private soldier in 1939 might have become an NCO, or been commissioned by 1945. Thirty are listed as Officer Cadets – of these we know that T. R. Burrows was a brigadier by the end of the war. Similarly, an initial rank of Leading Aircraftman in the Royal Air Force indicates an aircrew trainee: on completion of training and the award of the flying badge ('wings'), the rank of sergeant or pilot officer would be awarded – LAC G. C. Lamb became an Air Vice Marshal. I could identify at least 220 who held commissioned rank, without counting any of the sixty detailed above.

I discovered that almost 500 served in the army (43 in the King's Own, of whom 31 were commissioned.) Over 350 served in the various specialist corps (Artillery, Engineers, Electrical and Mechanical Engineers, Signals, Ordnance and Medical Corps). At least 285 were in the Royal Air Force, 75 as aircrew, of whom 40 lost their lives. At least 125 were in the Royal Navy, 14 as officers, with ten deaths. Of those who lost their lives, no fewer than 55 were listed as 'missing, believed killed'. At least 20 were decorated, seven receiving the Distinguished Flying Cross.

The Friends' School in Meeting House Lane was a private school, now 250 years old, while the Ripley Hospital was an orphanage foundation, accommodating and educating 300 boys and girls. In 1939 there was a proposal to close the orphanage and transfer the Boys' National School to the site. This was shelved, but was implemented after the war. The other elementary schools (five to fourteen years) were mostly Church of England schools of the National Society – the boys and girls National schools, and the parochial schools of St John, St Thomas, Christ Church, St Luke and Scotforth St Paul. The Roman Catholic Church had the Cathedral school of St Peter and the Skerton school of St Joseph, while board schools of Bowerham, Skerton, Marsh and (most recently) Greaves and Ryelands completed the roll. While many of these had rolls of honour from the First World War few seem to have such records from the Second. The exception is the Royal Grammar School, which added to its total of 78 killed from 1914 to 1918, no fewer than 118 from 1939 to 1945. A total of a thousand of its former pupils served, with about 250 being commissioned and at least 25 receiving decorations.

CHAPTER 11

HMS *LANCASTER*

THE fifth ship to bear the name HMS *Lancaster* was one of the 50 elderly destroyers of the US Navy transferred to the Royal Navy in 1940. She had been laid down at Bath Iron Works in Maine in September 1917, soon after the American entry into the war, and was commissioned on 24 August 1918 as USS *Philip* (DD76). Of 1100 tons, with a ship's company of 146, she mounted four 4" guns and one 3", with 21" torpedo tubes, and was capable of 35 knots. She joined Squadron 2, Cruiser Force, and was involved in convoy escort and anti-submarine patrol during the closing months of the war. In 1922 she was laid up.

The Royal Navy had begun the war with only 123 modern destroyers, barely enough for fleet and convoy escort duties, and twenty-eight of these had been lost in the first year of the war, largely in the Norwegian and Dunkirk campaigns. The American ships were old and in some respects unsuitable for action: they lacked ASDIC, radar and anti-aircraft and anti-submarine weapons. But they were a welcome addition, and seemed to presage a more active co-operation with the USA. They were renamed after towns and cities common to Britain and the USA, and the new HMS *Lancaster* was among the first batch to arrive in Portsmouth, with key American crew members aboard to ensure an efficient hand-over.

The city raised £31,000 towards re-equipment, and the ship was then pressed into service as a convoy escort, along with her sisters and their contemporaries of the V and W classes.

Lancaster was at first based in the Kyle of Lochalsh, as escort to the minelayers led by the cruiser HMS *Adventure*, which were then extending the northern barrage on minefields between Scotland and Norway, to confine the German fleet to the North Sea. Then, in May 1941, after a second refit, she was part of the escort for a convoy from Iceland. A further refit in the Humber equipped her with radar, and she served in the Atlantic and the Arctic, adding new battle honours to add to those won by her predecessors since 1694. The destroyer was formally 'adopted' by the city in 1942, in which year she escorted a Gibraltar-bound troop convoy during the build-up to Operation Torch, the allied invasion of French North Africa. Another refit in Belfast in 1943 gave her improved anti-aircraft armament in the shape of 20mm Oerlikon guns, and anti-submarine weaponry in depth charges. After a further spell with the minelaying force, she was transferred to the 17th Destroyer Flotilla, based in

USS *Philip* (DD76), which was transferred to the Royal Navy in 1940, and renamed HMS *Lancaster*.
US NAVAL WAR COLLEGE MUSEUM

Rosyth. When her sister, HMS *Rockingham*, struck a mine and sank in September, *Lancaster* rescued her crew. She continued in escort duties in the North Sea before, in 1945, being used as a target vessel in the Moray Forth by aircraft of the Fleet Air Arm.

She was paid off into the Reserve Fleet at the end of the war in Europe, and in 1947 was scrapped at Blyth. The silver American star from her funnel was preserved, and is borne by the Duke class frigate which now bears the name Lancaster.

BY UNKNOWN (ARTIST), J WEINER, LONDON (PRINTER), MINISTRY OF FOOD (PUBLISHER/SPONSOR),
HER MAJESTY'S STATIONERY OFFICE (PUBLISHER/SPONSOR) [PUBLIC DOMAIN], VIA WIKIMEDIA
COMMONS

CHAPTER 12

A CRITICAL YEAR

In 1941 Lancaster City Council sent a deputation to Merseyside to view the results of bombing in Birkenhead and Wallasey, and the work of the volunteer units there. They were shown the bomb damage, and the work done to rehouse those made homeless, and the arrangements for shelters. This was a continuing issue, with criticism of the slow progress made. There was so far provision for only 5,511 in street shelters and 5,630 in school shelters. What appeared to be a government poster on 'Health in your shelter' turned out to be another advertisement for Ovaltine.

Blood donations were sent to Manchester to supply transfusions there. In addition, the Lancaster Auxiliary Fire Service unit had been deployed in Manchester during air raids there, and an appreciative letter from the Lord Mayor of that city was read to the council. Later the award of the British Empire medal to Fireman G. Harrison was announced. The bombing there had a repercussion in an advertisement for Dents, the furniture shop in Penny Street. 'Our Manchester showrooms were burnt out last week, but our warehouse, containing the main stock was untouched. We therefore removed this Stock of High Grade Furniture to Lancaster to offer at one third below normal retail prices'.

In support of the 'Dig for Victory' campaign, seven sites were identified for use in growing vegetables. These included Ryelands Park, and the public playing fields on Willow Lane. The latter had been earmarked for the building of a new school, but that plan had been shelved 'for the duration' to quote the current phrase. Vegetables continued to loom large in the Ministry of Food posters. 'On the Kitchen Front' gave recipes for potato and carrot pancakes, savoury splits with chopped vegetable filling, and 'piccaninnies' – baked potatoes with – yes – a chopped vegetable filling.

A reduction in the milk ration was announced, taking effect from 13 April. The milk saved was to be made into cheese, or tinned to be put into store. Eggs were now rationed, with dried egg becoming an alternative to what became known as 'shell eggs' increasingly hard to come by. Clothes too were rationed from August, with sixty-six coupons allowing for the acquisition of one new outfit each year. The growth of the queue was noted. 'No sooner does word go round that a particular establishment has a certain commodity for sale, than people arrive from all quarters and form a queue'.

The Princess Royal visited Lancaster to inspect the ATS depot and its trainees. A services canteen was established in the YMCA premises in China Street, and was opened by Lady Ashton. The Spitfire Fund exceeded £2,000. The Council approved the purchase of steel helmets for the volunteers, distributed tons of sand and sold a quantity of stirrup pumps at £1.

An application was made for the formation of a squadron of the newly-established Air Training Corps. This became 345 (City of Lancaster) Squadron. Senior NCOs of the Officers' Training Corps at the Royal Grammar School proposed the formation of an ATC unit there, but the Headmaster instead arranged that there should be a Detached Flight at the School, run by members of the teaching staff. One of the NCOs was Cadet Sergeant G. C. Lamb of Hornby. He joined the RAF the following year, and trained as a pilot. He was a Flight Lieutenant at the end of the war, but went on to reach the rank of Air Vice Marshal.

A band was formed in 1943, and the following year it won the North West Region Challenge Cup at the Belle Vue Arena in

Manchester. The *Guardian* reported that almost all of its members were boarders of the Royal Grammar School in the detached flight. In 1942 a branch of the Women's Junior Air Corps was established, giving training to girls aged 16 to 18.

Tribunals continued to meet regularly in the Shire Court to hear applications for exemption from call-up. These covered the whole Lancaster area, in the Lune valley and Furness, and at one there were only five Lancaster men. Two were registered, with the proviso that they should be liable for non-combatant duties, and the other three appeals were rejected.

A government announcement extended Summer time (from May to August) to two hours – 'Double Summer Time'. The *Observer* editor commented that industrialists approved this, but the agricultural community did not. 'Mothers will not look favourably on this, as children are unwilling to go to bed while it is still light, and if they do, will not go to sleep'.

A remarkable advertisement appeared in April 1941. 'Don't let Hitler's fire bombs scare you', it began. 'The AGRIPPA incendiary bomb lifter will deal with this menace easily and effectively. Easy to use. More effective than sand. A saver of Life, Time, Property. Every home should have one. 16/9 from Attwaters in Cheapside'.

At the same time the irrepressible Colonel Ross (prospective Liberal candidate for the Lancaster Division) was at odds with his party and its leader over the duration of the present government. It had been agreed that unless some very drastic circumstances made it necessary, the present administration should continue in office until the end of the war. It had also been thought necessary to consider the advisability of its continuance after the war ended. The Colonel 'spoiling for a fight' wanted to see an election as soon as possible after hostilities ended, and before peace terms were discussed. (In the event, of course, an election was held soon after victory in Europe had been achieved.) The following month he addressed a meeting of the local Liberal party, saying that the present government was leading the country towards totalitarianism – 'the only real alternative to dictatorship in this country is a Liberal government'.

In June the Lancaster MP, Mr Herward Ramsbottom was raised to the peerage, taking his title from Soulbury, the Buckinghamshire village where he was born. This necessitated a by-election but it was a while before the writ was issued. This gave rise to a great deal of speculation about candidates. The main parties had all agreed not to oppose the government, so it was thought that the Conservative and Unionist candidate (since Lancaster was a conservative-held seat) would be elected unopposed. Colonel Ross, however, decided to put his name forward, but since this was against Liberal Party policy, he stood as an independent. There was talk of a candidate from the National Farmers' Union, but the Union decided that it had insufficient notice to participate while Mr Fenner Brockway, a member of the Independent Labour Party, also stood as a candidate. He campaigned solely on the grounds of a minimum wage of £3, while Colonel Ross pledged 'a healthy stimulus' by criticism of the government. Mr F. H. McLean was the Conservative party candidate, and not initially supported by the government, so the Liberal party decided that it could support Colonel Ross but both the Prime Minister and the Foreign Secretary, Mr Anthony Eden wrote to Mr McLean, pledging government support. The election was held with little of the usual enthusiasm – 'no favours, no cars with posters of the candidate' and there was only a 41 per cent turnout. Mr McLean won with 15,783 votes, Colonel Ross securing 6,551 and Mr Fenner Brockway third with 5,418.

A parade of tanks through the streets was the prelude to another appeal, with a target of £15,000 per week (enough to pay for a medium tank) for the next eight weeks. A dramatic picture of a Matilda tank crossing the Lune was published.

In October one may note that, showing at the Palladium, was *The Road to Zanzibar* starring Bob Hope, Bing Crosby and Dorothy Lamour, attired in her usual risqué sarong. The County had James

Stewart and Hedy Lamar in *Come Live with Me* and the Odeon Vivien Leigh and Laurence Olivier in *Lady Hamilton*. The Grand Theatre screened *I Married a Millionaire*, with Sonje Henie and Don Ameche.

Gifts from America under the scheme called 'Bundles for Britain' arrived for children in the RLI who had been wounded in bombing raids in big cities, but all too soon the USA became directly involved in the war with the Japanese raid on Pearl Harbor. 'We want to know how our American allies will respond,' wrote the editor of the *Guardian*. 'Our first enemy remains Hitler, but our Russian allies are hitting back hard, and in the middle east our own forces are obtaining the ascendancy'.

Tank Week 1941, in Dalton Square
(LG/LCM) COURTESY OF LANCASTER CITY MUSEUM PART OF LANCASHIRE MUSEUMS

BY UNKNOWN (ARTIST), STAFFORD AND CO, NETHERFIELD, NOTTINGHAM (PRINTER),
MINISTRY OF FOOD (PUBLISHER/SPONSOR), HER MAJESTY'S STATIONERY OFFICE
(PUBLISHER/SPONSOR) [PUBLIC DOMAIN], VIA WIKIMEDIA COMMONS

CHAPTER 13

THE TURN OF THE TIDE

'WE entered 1942 in a much more confident state of mind than we did last year' claimed the editor of the *Observer*. Victory has been brought appreciably nearer by the events of the last six months. The involvement of the United States in the war, and the passage of the Lease-Lend bill were two of these events, but the extent of early Japanese success was not anticipated. The news of the loss of Hong Kong and Singapore, and the sinking of Force Z were concealed for weeks until there was cautious reference to 'outposts of empire which we had thought impregnable have crumbled under the enemy's attacks'. Shipping losses were also rising with the deployment of 'wolf packs' of German submarines in the Atlantic.

Paper salvage again became the subject of a campaign to collect £20,000 worth of newspapers, books and magazines, while an even more ambitious target was set for Warship Week – £700,000 to build a destroyer. In the event £621,000 was raised. A system of paper rationing led to the reduction of the size of the local newspapers from eight pages to six.

Increasingly the Anglo-Soviet Friendship Society was getting publicity from lectures and meetings involving the Labour Party and the Trades Council, with great stress on Russia's resistance to Germany.

In mid-1942 the Ministry of Food's 'Food Facts' showed two new developments. One, headed 'Man-about-Kitchen' pointed out that 'as thousands of wives and mothers are working in factories, men are having to do the cooking' and offered two easy recipes – for brisket of beef and for parsnip savoury (essentially parsnips, carrots and rasher of bacon). For good measure, 'wash day rules' were added. A later bulletin dealt with dried eggs 'which have the same food value as shell eggs, but, as the yolk and white are mixed, cannot be boiled, poached or fried'. A Potato County Championship was announced, with counties such as Devon, Hampshire and Surrey being challenged to beat Lancashire hot pot for the title.

From 11 July, chocolate and sweets were rationed, 'personal points' allowing 8 ounces per month. The rationing of coal was anticipated. In the later months of the year, fund-raising was a major pre-occupation. The workforce of Lansil, having already raised £5,000 in War Weapons Week, now added a further £2,000 in Tank Week. Then an ambitious target of £250,000 for a Lancaster bomber 'as a Christmas present for the RAF' fell only a little short, the fund closing at £210,707.

Scrap metal 'to build a battleship' was sought, with the city's iron railings being the first to go (though there were claims of unnecessary damage). Non-ferrous metals, brass, copper, pewter, tin and lead could also be handed in to a depot in New Street.

The Council also voted to send, to each of the 4,000 men and women serving in the armed forces, a Christmas card from the Mayor and a postal order for 2s. 6d., in addition to the 2,000 parcels already dispatched.

CHAPTER 14

MILITARY SUCCESS

1943 opened on a much more cheerful note, with news of successes, especially in North Africa, with the surrender of 150,000 Axis troops in Tunisia. The now traditional New Year party for evacuees was held in the Town Hall, with their foster parents also in attendance. The Odeon was showing *Desert Victory*, while at the Palace one might view *Random Harvest* with Greer Garson and Ronald Coleman. Greer Garson was also starring at the Palladium, along with Walter Pigeon in *Mrs Miniver*.

The expected rationing of coal took place, and economy in the use of gas and electricity was urged. The innovation of utility furniture was announced. This could only be purchased by those holding a ministry permit, normally only issued to those with a special need. These were principally those who had lost furniture in bombing raids or couples about to marry. An indication that invasion was no longer a threat was the restoration of road signs. A relaxation of blackout regulations allowed improved lighting in railway trains and on vehicles.

The Squanderbug made his first appearances on government posters, urging people to waste money or commodities – a typically English use of irony.

Since the Cardwell reforms of the 1880s, Lancaster had had its own regiment, the King's Own, and in both world wars a ship of the Royal Navy had borne the city's name. Now 77 Squadron Royal Air Force was adopted, to become 77 (City of Lancaster) Squadron.

FANCY TRYING TO MEND THAT OLD THING!

HE HATES TO SEE CLOTHES DOING EXTRA WAR SERVICE

This kind of war work drives the Squander Bug wild! Don't listen to him . . . keep right on with it. You'll be as proud as punch of your 'creations' —no cash or coupons required. Now you will be able to buy more Savings Certificates . . . no wonder the Squander Bug hates that sewing machine!

Savings Certificates costing 15/- are worth 20/6 in 10 years—increase free of income tax. They can be bought outright, or by instalments with 6d., 2/6 or 5/- Savings Stamps through your Savings Group or Centre or at any Post Office or Trustee Savings Bank. Buy now!

ISSUED BY THE NATIONAL SAVINGS COMMITTEE

Now re-equipped with Lancaster bombers, she was commanded by Wing Commander A. C. Lewis, who was, unusually, an air gunner. All three adopted units took part in the parades which, in May, marked 'Wings for Victory Week'. Roy Chadwick, designer of the Lancaster bomber, opened the proceedings, and a Lancaster was on display throughout the week. An ambitious target of £500,000 had been set, and a host of fund-raising activities took place. Concerts, dances, whist drives, a swimming gala and a water polo match were staged, as well as a baseball match between American and Canadian personnel. The Central Band of the Royal Air Force gave a concert in the Town Hall (tickets at 3s. 6d., 2s. and 1s.). An exhibition of photographs of all serving personnel was held, and the Co-operative Society at its AGM voted £50,000 to start the fund. In the event the target was comfortably exceeded, with £676,515 the eventual total.

About this time (for security reasons there was no mention in the press) departments of the Canadian Treasury were evacuated to Lancaster, after being bombed out of their London premises. Here to deal with pay and allowances for Canadian troops already stationed in England for the forthcoming invasion of Europe, they were accommodated in the County and King's Arms hotels. They employed some local people, including my informant and his wife. The wedding of Corporal D. W. Digby of the Royal Canadian Army Pay Corps to Miss E. Lamb of Oxford Street was one result.

Two unusual items of news were given photographs in mid-1943. Bruno, the Alsatian dog at the Moorlands Hotel was given his 'call-up' papers, while the wedding of Miss Evelyn Victoria Knowles to Corporal L. Henge of the American army made her Lancaster's first 'GI Bride' (a term not yet in use). A Lancaster woman, Miss Elsie Slinger of Newsham Road had been working for the NAAFI at a north-west camp, but had then been posted to North Africa.

By this time, with Russian advances in the east, and the allied invasion of Sicily, it could be said that the war 'had turned the corner'. The collapse of Italy and her joining the allied side after the fall of Mussolini gave rise to much jubilation, and occasioned the return of allied prisoners of war. It was not then realised how stubborn would be the resistance of the German forces in that country.

Wings for Victory Week 1943
(LG/LCM) COURTESY OF LANCASTER CITY MUSEUM PART OF LANCASHIRE MUSEUMS

The changed position in the Mediterranean enabled the import of fruit from Turkey, Sicily and North Africa, and Lord Woolton, Minister of Food, announced that dried fruit would be available by Christmas, and that home production of foodstuffs was three times the figure for 1942. The first lemons reached Lancaster in January 1944.

Mid-September saw the inaugural Battle of Britain services in all Lancaster churches. The Mayor and Corporation attended the

Priory and Parish church, with a large-scale parade afterwards. The band of the King's Own led members of the RAF, WAAF, Home Guard, Royal Observer Corps, ACF, ATC, British Legion, National Fire Service, ARP Wardens, St John's Ambulance Brigade, nurses, Women's Land Army, Scouts, Guides and Church Lads' Brigade, with a Wing Commander of the RAF taking the salute on the steps of the Town Hall.

A renewed salvage drive saw schools involved for the first time, and an appeal for 100,000 books brought 40,000 in the first week, and 146,147 in total. These were distributed to libraries which had lost stock through bombing, to hospitals, and to the services, with unwanted books pulped for salvage. The City Librarian was assisted by a team led by the local author Garry Hogg.

Five repatriated prisoners of war, led by CQMS G. Denwood (Royal Engineers) of Friar Street were given a civic reception at the Town Hall, where all paid thanks to the Red Cross whose food parcels had made life in the camps more endurable.

The local Member of Parliament was in the headlines again after a speech by the foreign secretary in the House of Commons. Now a Brigadier, F. H. McLeod was a leader of the British mission to Yugoslavia, working alongside General Tito, leader of the partisans there. He also received a Soviet decoration from Stalin.

CHAPTER 15

VICTORY IN SIGHT

In 1944, the government was beginning to look to post-war work, with the publication of Mr R. A. Butler's Education Bill. The local reaction concerned the transfer of control from boroughs to county councils, rather than the introduction of a tripartite system of grammar, technical and modern schools. Similarly the white paper introducing a National Health Service was greeted with alarm about the end of the volunteer hospital, such as the Lancaster Royal Infirmary. A new 'pay as you earn' tax system was also anticipated.

A Council Committee or post-war reconstruction began its deliberations. In Lancaster there was not the urgent need for replacement of bombed homes, but the provision of new houses was still a priority, together with new schools, roads and bridges. Tenders were sought for the building of a nursery at Greaves Park.

In May came the next big fund-raising project – 'Salute the Soldier Week'. With the invasion of Europe expected shortly, the council set a target of £700,000. The week began with the usual parade, led by the band of the King's Own, with troops, Civil Defence workers, Home Guard, nurses, Women's Land Army, cadets, scouts and guides following. An extensive programme included a display of military vehicles and weapons, a boxing tournament (army versus RAF personnel), a swimming gala in the Kingsway Baths, a Norwegian girls' ball game on Giant Axe field, a variety show and a final ball in the Ashton Hall. The huge sum of £775,432 was raised.

In the same month an inquest returned a verdict of accidental death on Sapper W. Bollen, drowned when a Churchill tank under test after repairs, plunged into the Lune at Halton Camp. Tests were also being held to check the suitability of Scale Hall for a landing site for RAF aircraft.

The news both of the D-Day landings and the liberation of Rome was greeted by the *Observer* with great satisfaction, though with a note of caution about the likely casualty list. (The *Guardian* made no mention of either event.) However the same issue of the *Observer* had more to say about juvenile crime. This had been a recurrent theme

Salute the Soldier parade 1944
(LG/LCM) COURTESY OF LANCASTER CITY MUSEUM PART OF LANCASHIRE MUSEUMS

ATS canteen in Salvation Army premises, 1940

since the outbreak of war, but was now treated at greater length. 'The frequency with which children of tender years make their appearance before magistrates, and the air of unconcern with which they and their parents face the issue is most exasperating, particularly to those who have to deal with them. It must be brought home to young people that thieving is a serious crime, and that parents, are mistaken in being so often prepared to condone their actions out of a sense of loyalty to their offspring'. At this time it was suggested that the term 'Police Courts' was misleading, and that they should be renamed 'Magistrates' Courts'. While looking for war news it was easy to be side-tracked by such headings as 'Elderly lady stole cake from pram' or 'Woman knocked down by cow'.

More war news was now available, under the heading 'Now it can be told'. Lance Corporal G. Poles of the King's Own told how, after the cruiser HMS *Manchester* had been struck on the port side by a torpedo from an Italian aircraft, he and his colleagues had been involved in transferring stores to starboard to correct the ship's list

before she limped back to Gibraltar for repairs. Stoker B. Kelly of Moorlands had served aboard a Hunt class destroyer since she was first commissioned. The ship had sunk two submarines, had shot down five aircraft and, most remarkably, had accepted the surrender of a Sicilian town after a bombardment. He had served in her in the Arctic, the North Sea, the Atlantic and the Mediterranean. AB J. Bettany was serving in the destroyer HMS *Saumarez* when she torpedoed the German battlecruiser *Scharnhorst*. This slowed the enemy vessel so that she came under the 14" guns of the battleship Duke of York and was sunk off North Cape in December 1943, A visit to the city was made by Surgeon-Lieutenant C. R. Knappett, of HMS *Lancaster* to thank the women of the Queen Street Women's Institute for the knitted jerseys, scarves and gloves which they had provided for the ship's company. He was given a picture of old Lancaster for the ship.

A vivid letter from a corporal of the RAMC was published. He had gone ashore on D-Day, and had chronicled his experiences then and during the next fortnight. Another escaped PoW, Private D. Slack of Salisbury Road arrived back in Lancaster and told his story. Captured at Tobruk in 1942, he had been in an Italian PoW camp in Libya for six months. While subsequently being transported to Italy, his ship was torpedoed and he spent six hours in the water before being picked up by an Italian destroyer, where he was given coffee, but no food. In his new camp, there was no distribution of the Red Cross parcels, and, lacking food and medical supplies, many prisoners died from dysentery. Like others, he took advantage of the confusion in September 1943, to escape and make his way to the advancing British forces.

In the summer of 1944 the attacks on London brought a new wave of evacuated mothers and children – some 800 in all. Fortunately the arrangements which had been made by the billeting officer in 1939 stood, and enough volunteer householders offered accommodation. They all returned home within the year, the final

WVS mobile canteen – the gift of Lady Ashton

group of 151 leaving the Castle railway station in June 1945. An eyewitness account of 'Life in Bomb Alley' described the raids by the latest German weapon, the pilotless V1 'flying bombs'.

In July women over eighteen, whether single or married, with or without children, were required to register for war service unless already serving in the armed forces, in nursing or other medical work. They faced possible enlistment, though in practice only single women were called up.

Better news was that of the allied landings in the south of France, though this had to compete with the amalgamation, in August 1944, of the two local newspapers. Published under their joint names, the editorial comment called 'Observations' survived, as did the *Guardian's* 'Nig-Nog' page and the dress patterns of the inimitable Madame Doreen.

One of the early items of news was the welcome reduction of the hours of duty of the Civil Defence teams in those areas (including Lancaster) which had not been subjected to air raids. The only attacks now were by the unmanned V1 'Flying bombs', and their range was limited to London and the south-east. Black-out restrictions were also lifted, and the council proposed to run buses after 10 p.m.

The council's Housing Committee continued its post-war planning by disclosing its plans for 950 houses on the Ridge estate, with a community centre, a church, branch library and reading room and shops. The disused Customs House on the Quay was made over to LADOS (the Lancaster Dramatic and Operatic Society) as a club room, rehearsal room and properties store, a use which continued until its conversion into the city's Maritime Museum.

At the end of the year one could view *Rebecca*, starring Laurence Olivier and Joan Fontaine, at the Palace in Dalton Square, *The Song of Bernadette*, with Jennifer Jones at the Odeon, or Bing Crosby and Dorothy Lamour in *Dixie* at the Palladium, with its added attraction of its café.

Memorial plaques, Lancaster Priory

CHAPTER 16

1945

THE proposed change of name from Police Courts to Magistrates' courts took effect.

A meeting of the Lancaster branch of the Anglo-Russian Allied Friendship Society at the Storey Institute was addressed by an attaché from the Soviet Embassy.

Members of the crew of HMS *Lancaster* presented a plaque to the Queen Street WI, which had adopted the ship.

With the news that a General Election would follow the end of the war in Europe, a good deal of party political activity took place. Candidates were adopted and meetings held to publicise policy. Although the Labour Party won nationally, in Lancaster the sitting Conservative member, Brigadier F. H. R. McLean, held his seat with 27,090 votes on a 74 per cent poll, a majority of 7,732. Mr E. A. V. A. Fraser (Labour) took second place with 19,367 votes, and Captain E. S. T. Johnson (Liberal) polled 8,357.

By then VE Day had been celebrated with a largely informal response. Street parties were held almost everywhere, despite rationing. The Mayor and Corporation attended a service of thanksgiving at the Priory Church, but the subsequent military parade on Giant Axe Field had to be cut short because of a heavy downpour. The *Guardian* was highly critical of the 'low-key' celebrations, contending that the end of the war had been in sight for long enough for better preparations to have been made – though no suggestions were offered.

Lancaster War Memorial, to the side of the Town Hall

CHAPTER 17

PEACE AT LAST

THE end of the war in the Far East came with dramatic suddenness with the dropping of the atomic bombs on Hiroshima and Nagasaki, but the *Guardian* was highly critical of the council's response, as it had been after VE Day. Public buildings were decorated, the War Memorial was floodlit, bands played in Dalton Square, and the Mayor and Corporation attended a service in the Priory Church. But there was 'nothing of a ceremonial nature. For the rest they were content to leave their fellow citizens to celebrate final victory just as they chose'. The informal celebrations 'turned night into day, with music, singing, dancing and bonfires', though this report was flanked by a Ministry of Food 'Food Facts' panes, on 'Making the Most of Cabbage' – a reminder that rationing was to remain in force during years of austerity. There was no suggestion as to what more might then have been arranged, but the fellow citizens had some idea. Street parties were held in the Westfield Memorial Village, on St George's Quay and the Marsh, and on Avondale Road, Ullswater Road and Edward Street. There was the now traditional Remembrance Sunday in November, and a memorial service for the King's Own dead of both wars.

In the final months of 1945, there came a steady stream of returning prisoners of war from Japanese camps, but also belated news of some who had died in captivity. These included Sergeant E. Simpson of the Royal Artillery and Private C. Ryan of the

Manchester Regiment who lost their lives when the Japanese transport conveying them from Thailand was sunk.

However, Captain R. G. Swainson (88 Field Regiment), Royal Artillery and Lieutenant Colonel G. E. C. Rossall RASC, both taken at the fall of Singapore, were among those returning.

The council placed its first housing tender, for 72 houses to be built on the Hare Runs estate, with another 64 to follow. In addition, the Minister of Health allocated 100 factory built houses to Lancaster. These 'pre-fabs' were sited on Ashton Road, opposite the Ripley Hospital, and were still in use in the mid-'60s, when they were replaced by bungalows of a very similar design. The demolition of the street air raid shelters was held to be a matter of urgency, but by the end of 1946, nothing had been done.

Alderman T. W. Helme proposed a war memorial with a community use, along the lines of the Westfield Memorial Village, but this met with spirited opposition from a lady of 90, who wrote to the *Guardian* imagining the reaction of those who had lost sons 'to see them commemorated in a hall where every conceivable frivolity is going on'.

After the First World War, besides the main memorial by the Town Hall, with 1008 names of the fallen, churches, firms, schools, sports clubs and other organisations had their own memorials, splendidly catalogued by the Lancaster Military Heritage Group. Only a few added a new list of names for 1939–'45. One exception is, of course, the city memorial where an altar-like stone was added, with a plaque bearing 328 names – less than a third of those who had died in the first war.

At the Royal Grammar School a new plaque bearing 118 names was added to the Memorial Library. Not all of these were Lancaster men; some will have been day boys from the Lune valley, and others boarders from East Lancashire or elsewhere. Only eight other memorials have a 1939–'45 addition: these are Greaves Methodist

Church (24 names), St Joseph's RC Church (21), Standfast (14), Gillows (11), the Co-op (9), Phoenix Street WMC (7), Moor Hospital (6) and the GPO (2).

CHAPTER 18

RECOLLECTIONS

Mʀs Eunice Howard (née Blenkarn), then living in Middle Street, Dry Dock, and a pupil at Christ Church CE School, recalls the air raid siren on 3 September, announcing the outbreak of war – she was eight years old.

Everyone was issued with a gas mask, and told to carry it at all times, and with an identity card – mine was number NMVR 65/3. At first when the sirens sounded, we used to go down into the cellar, where we were joined by an elderly neighbour, and later a brick shelter was built in the middle of the street. After a while, as no bombs dropped on Lancaster, we just stayed in bed.

My dad was an engine driver – a reserved occupation – so my mother decided to 'do her bit' and went to work at Gillows, as a machinist. She made camouflage nets, tents and canvas coffins. Elsewhere in the factory, cutting blocks for Navy butchers, oak tables for RAF Officers' Messes, and trestle tables for other ranks were made. Later, wings for the wooden Mosquito aircraft were produced.

A Canadian soldier from Halton Camp became a friend of the family, and his mother sent us a food parcel, with biscuits, chocolates and a whole tinned chicken. On my thirteenth birthday he gave me a large parcel, with layer upon layer of wrapping, which at last revealed a pound note – a fortune in 1943.

Clothing coupons were treasured like gold, and clogs became fashionable – mine were green.

VE Day 1945 was my fifteenth birthday, the street lights came on and there were street parties and a coach trip to the Lake District in an ancient coach which had been laid up for the duration of the war.

Another contributor writes:

> I was only two when the war began, and my principal recollections concern rationing. My mother and I (father was in the army) were entitled to a pound of jam between us each month, and it was always red plum. I have not eaten red plum jam since 1945. Then instead of what were called 'shell eggs', we had dried egg substitute, adequate for an omelette, but no substitute for a real breakfast boiled egg. For breakfast mother would make what were called bacon cakes – small patties of flour, water and salt, fried in the fat of our shared rasher of bacon. But the worst of all was the butter ration. This was 3 ounces each per week, and to save waste, the grocer would give us a half pound block in alternate weeks, with a mere four ounces in intervening weeks – the 'little butter weeks'.

> After the war, there was not only a continuation of rationing, with bread and potatoes (not rationed during the war) added to the list in 1947, but also real austerity, with goods being 'in short supply' or 'for export only'. New cars were almost unobtainable, and my father bought a 1934 Morris 8 for £105. The next year he acquired a beautiful 1932 Sunbeam 12 saloon.

Bob Rowley, who died in 1994 at Scaleford Nursing Home, lived in Dorrington Road during the war, and worked for the Canadian Treasury at the old County Hotel opposite the Castle Station. His wife worked with the billeting office for evacuees, and they accommodated two of them for some months.

One former evacuee from Salford wrote to me about his experiences.

> Immediately on the outbreak of war, trainloads of school-age children from Salford were sent northwards for safety. At Lancaster those over eleven alighted, while younger children (including my brother and sisters) went on to Ulverston. We boarded corporation buses at the Castle Station, and were driven to Bowerham, where the billeting officer led us up Coulston Road, knocking on doors and asking the householders if they would accommodate one or (preferably) two of us. I was fortunate in that a friend and I were taken in by a very pleasant couple – a police inspector and his wife. We pupils of Salford Grammar School shared the laboratories and sports facilities of Lancaster Royal

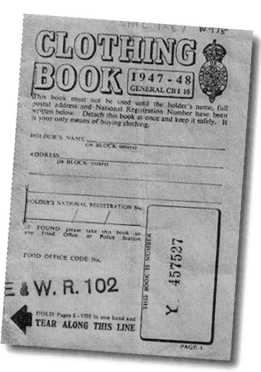

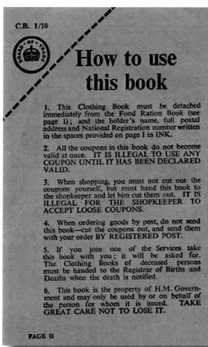

Grammar School, using rooms at the nearby Gregson Institute as classrooms.

By Christmas there had been no bombing, and most of us returned home, but when raids began in the autumn of 1940, my mother did not wait for the official process, but contacted the couple I had stayed with, and I remained with them until the end of the war, the other Salford evacuees returned home in 1943, but I transferred to become a pupil at the Royal Grammar School.

Margaret Shaw lived first on Chester Place in Bowerham, but when her father was due to be called up, the family rented the house to a couple from Manchester, and they lived for a while with an aunt and uncle in South Road. It was there, in 1941 that they watched her father walking away to join up, tears running down her mother's face. They later moved to live with another aunt, and her grandad, in Bridge Road where they remained for the rest of the war. There were a lot of children in the area, and they played outside for much of the time – hopscotch, tag, skipping and whips and tops. She has many happy memories of the years, despite the war – her uncle made her a doll's house complete with furniture, and a farm complete with

animals. One Christmas she had a bicycle, and she rode with her mother out to Conder Green. A cousin worked at Gillows, making the wooden fuselages for Mosquito aircraft, and she made the six-year old Margaret a wiggly snake.

She started at Bowerham School in 1941, aged five, in a class of fifty-two (not unusual for those days). Though her teacher, Mrs Richardson, was very strict, she made bonfire toffee with sugar provided by the mothers of the pupils (no bonfires or fireworks, of course). The walk to school, up Bridge Road and Sharpe's Hill, then along Lonsdale Place and Parkfield Road had to be done three times a day, rain, hail or shine. Bowerham barracks was just opposite the school, and she recalls watching soldiers drive tanks over an artificial mound.

An air raid scare one night had them going downstairs and piling bedding on the dining table, but it proved to be the noise of a light engine in the nearby railway track.

Margaret had mixed experiences with evacuees. The first, Steve, in 1939 stole the keys to her father's safe where he kept the insurance money he collected, and left under a cloud. A brother and sister, Norman and Mavis, had nits, so there was a nightly ritual with a comb and vinegar. Another, Eunice, was very happy in Lancaster and cried when she had to return to Salford, but she and Margaret kept in touch until Eunice died in September 2016.

When the war ended her father was posted to Germany, not being demobilised until 1946, when life returned to normal.

A later survey by Sue Ashworth revealed a wide variety of experience among the evacuees. The lucky ones found good homes, with loving foster-parents, some of whom wished to adopt their charges. One or two, allocated to wealthy families, saw a glimpse of a better life than they had experienced in the slum areas of Salford. Others were treated harshly, even cruelly, and were convinced that they had been taken in purely for the financial allowances paid. Those from good homes, allocated to slum areas, to overcrowded houses lacking amenities such as running water and indoor lavatories found life bleak and harsh.

Alan Duckworth, in his illustrated booklet 'Light on Old Lancaster', records that on Easter Monday, 1941, children parading in the Barton Road playing fields ran for cover when a German aircraft was seen overhead. It was later shot down near Silloth on the Solway Firth, where there was an RAF training station.

CHAPTER 19

1946

THE serious shortage of food plagued every life. The reduction in size of the standard loaf was intended to make the grain supply go further, while a fifteen per cent reduction in the production of beer enabled the barley saved to go to famine-struck Europe. The Ministry of Food explained 'How to get your new ration book' in newspaper advertisements, while bread and potato rationing was implemented (they had never been rationed during the war). Re-registration for milk supply was also required, while coal supplies for household use remained limited.

Throughout the year, housing was the main priority for the city council, but progress was slow. There were 1,890 families on the council's waiting list for houses in March, and, while the development of the Hare Runs estate had begun, the much bigger scheme for the Ridge was still in the future. There were several schemes for aluminium dwellings, and several applications were made for pre-fabs, fifty of which were erected on the Newton estate. An application was made to the Ministry of Health for a further seventy-five for Ryelands Road, and five new cottages (named after Second World War battles) were built at the Westfield Memorial Village. Meanwhile there were 'squatters' (commonplace at this time) occupying Lunecliffe in Ashton-with-Stodday, Laurel Bank on Cannon Hill, and Greaves House.

The County's Education Committee published its plans for the reorganisation of secondary education in Lancaster in the tripartite

Children's community singing, Dalton Square, Lancaster
COURTESY OF LANCASHIRE COUNTY COUNCIL

system laid down by the Butler Education Act of 1944, which also involved an increase in the school-leaving age to fifteen. There were to be extensions to the Royal Grammar School and the Girls' Grammar School to provide for 750 and 510 pupils respectively. A Technical School for 420 was to be built at Scale Hall, and the Central Schools, now called Secondary Modern Schools were to be expanded. Skerton Boys' School was to move to Powderhouse Lane, with the girls moving into its former premises. A new Dallas Road School was to be built on Caton Road, and Greaves School would move to Barton Road. Finally, the Boys' National School and St Thomas's School would move to the Ripley site, the orphanage having closed. Financial stringency meant that none of these plans was implemented, except the last which cost nothing in new building. The weak link in the Tripartite system was always the provision of technical education. The Junior Technical School at the Storey Institute had taken entrants at thirteen, when that was the school leaving age in the elementary schools, but what was wanted now was a secondary technical school taking pupils at eleven.

The government announced a Victory Day on 8 May, the Saturday of the Whit weekend, with a big parade and festivities in London, but Lancaster, like many other cities and towns, deemed this inappropriate in a time of austerity, though services were held in the city churches. A reminder that rationing was still in force was provided by the continuing 'Food Facts' panels provided by the Ministry of Food. The recipe for Creamed Egg Savoury required four ounces of dried eggs.

In December, Ripley Hospital reopened as a Teacher Training College, under the Emergency Teaching Plan, with a Principal, 19 staff and 240 ex-service students enrolled for a one-year course. Again the cry for the establishment of a University of Lancaster, already voiced several times earlier in the year, was raised. It would eventually come about, but not for another two decades.

In the same month, the city's MP, Brigadier McLean asked

a question in the House of Commons about the two hotels (the King's Arms and the County), which had been commandeered by the Home Office to house the UK branch of the Canadian Treasury. Although empty, these had not been returned to their owners, and there was a shortage of hotel accommodation in the city as a result. He did not get an altogether satisfactory reply: there was a possibility that they would be used as hostels for civil servants.

The Society of Friends held a meeting to urge the repatriation of German prisoners of war, of whom there were about 200,000 in the country. Only a few hundred had been released for special reasons. It was felt that they were being held as cheap labour, especially in agriculture, and the meeting resolved that this policy should be overturned. Locally there had been a camp for Italian prisoners at Bela River, near Milnthorpe, and there must have been many working on local farms.

BIBLIOGRAPHY

Books

Ashworth Sue (ed.), *The evacuees story* (Lancaster City Museum: Lancaster, 1999).

Fidler John, *Lancaster in the Great War* (Pen & Sword: Barnsley, 2016).

Fidler John, *Lancaster Royal Grammar School* (Governors of the School: Lancaster, 2011).

Fidler John, *HMS Lancaster 1694–2011* (Lancaster Maritime Museum: Lancaster, 2011).

Purdy Martin, *Westfield Memorial Village*: disability, paternalism and philanthropy, 1915-2015 (Lancaster University, 2017).

Swain Robert, *Lancaster – a History and Celebration* (Francis Frith: Gillingham, 2004).

White Andrew, *Lancaster – a History* (Phillimore: Bognor Regis, 2003).

White Andrew (ed.), *A History of Lancaster* (Ryburn: Keele, 1993).

Newspapers and periodicals

File copies of *Lancaster Guardian* and *Lancaster Observer* 1937–46.

The Lancastrian – Magazine of Lancaster Royal Grammar School 1939–46.

THE AUTHOR

JOHN Fidler was born in Northumberland in 1936, and was educated at Carlisle Grammar School and at Keble College, Oxford, where he read History. He taught this subject at Lancaster Royal Grammar School from 1962–97, subsequently acting as Admissions Tutor until 2013. During his National service he held an aircrew commission in the Royal Air Force, training in Canada as a navigator, and then served with the LRGS contingent of the Combined Cadet Force, establishing an RAF Section in 1964. He later commanded the contingent for fifteen years in the rank of Wing Commander.

He has published a history of LRGS, a book on the development of the battleship from 1820 to 1945, and 'Lancaster in the Great War'.